CW01628935

HASHIMOTO'S THYROIDITIS

A guide for the newly diagnosed to reduce symptoms, increase energy and reclaim your life.

Adele Du Rand

Cover designed by Debbie Boettcher
debbieboettcher@absamail.co.za
Layout by Kim Hunter
www.datewithabook.co.za

Printed in South Africa

ISBN
(print) 978-1-928533-51-1
(ebook) 978-1-928533-52-8

CONTENTS

PREMISE

Hashimoto's Thyroiditis

- An autoimmune disease that has been undiagnosed by your doctor, likely for years, while you have been struggling with the symptoms of an underactive thyroid.
- Despite taking your prescription thyroid medication, you have not been feeling like a normal person who has the energy to do every day, normal things. In fact, most days have been a struggle just to get through the day.
- You just have no idea if there is anything that you can do to feel better, think more clearly and regain energy to live your best life.
- You have been gaining weight while losing energy, and nothing seems to help.
- Your doctor has tested your thyroid and told you it is within the normal ranges. Or you have been told "*it's in your head*".

Here are the facts to consider.

You have an autoimmune disease that has no known cure (yet). However, you can live a great life with limitless energy despite having

Hashimoto's Thyroiditis. Regaining your health and your life is simple, but it is not always easy.

This book is written specifically to make it easier for you.

MY REASON FOR WRITING THIS BOOK

My mission is to help *you*, who has been diagnosed with Hashimoto's Thyroiditis, and to help you claim back your energy so you are able to live a fulfilling and rewarding life.

Hashimoto's Thyroiditis is an autoimmune disease that can take everything from you: your energy, your mind, your willpower, your drive, and even your personality. In simple terms, it consumes your life. It can cause anxiety and depression, and it can make you question your own sanity. It can cause an emotional rollercoaster ride not just for you, but also for your family and your friends. The lack of energy you are experiencing is not "*in your head*" and it is not just about "*getting over yourself*". It is real, and the struggle is extremely real.

I have Hashimoto's Thyroiditis. Over the years I have taken my thyroid medication exactly as my doctor advised me to, and yet I still didn't have energy to play with my daughter, pursue my career ambitions, visit with friends, and even enjoy intimacy with my husband. I witnessed the energetic, love-life-and-adventure person that I used to be, disappearing. This autoimmune disease has taken a substantial amount from my life - but not anymore.

I have, and still am, taking my health back. And you can too. This is my story.

MY STORY

I probably already had Hashimoto's Thyroiditis when I was first diagnosed with an underactive thyroid in 2003, at the age of 27. I started studying for an MBA part-time while working full-time as an investment analyst. I loved my work, and I was working long hours with hectic deadlines. Asking for help wasn't something I did easily, as I thought that high performers just "*got the work done*".

February 2003 was a stressful time, as I had just started studying in the MBA programme with the University of Pretoria. Between working and studying, I thought the tiredness I felt was due to a lack of sleep and the workload. However, the tiredness persisted. It became so severe that even after sleeping for 10 hours a night, I would wake up feeling like a deflated balloon. I would go to work and when I arrived home in the late afternoon, would lie down on the couch and fall asleep. Johann, my husband, would arrive home, make dinner and wake me up to eat. After dinner, I would change into my pyjamas and go to bed to sleep. This continued for a few weeks. Something was definitely wrong.

I made an appointment with my doctor and explained the tiredness and the excessive sleeping. She ordered blood tests, and after a few days I received the results. My thyroid was underactive, and I was also deficient in iron. She started me on thyroid hormone replacement therapy (T4 only), a chelated iron formulation and gave me instructions to manage my stress.

That was the start of a very long journey to understanding what was wrong with me.

Over the next few years, the level of thyroid medication needed to be adjusted frequently. Sometimes the doctor had to increase the dosage, and other times we had to decrease the dosage. Every time I experienced different symptoms from being emotional, to my hair falling out, nails breaking easily, and struggled to keep weight off. In hindsight, I now know that during this time I had Hashimoto's Thyroiditis flare-ups.

It was towards the end of 2012 and I was finishing an 18-month long project. Working as a management consultant, I was part of the change management team on a project with a client that implemented SAP globally. This was a great project, and I loved being on site with the client and working with amazing people in Australia and the USA. It was during the week after the official go-live of SAP that everything hit me: I was emotional, and I experienced feelings of helplessness and of being overwhelmed. A colleague suggested that I should go and see my doctor as something clearly was not right. I made an appointment and I clearly remember walking into her rooms and just bursting into tears! After an examination she booked me off for the week, and we had everything re-tested. The thyroid hormones prescribed where now too high, which meant I was experiencing an over-active thyroid. She immediately decreased the medication accordingly. During December 2012 I rested and started feeling better. In March 2013 we re-tested the thyroid levels, and this time the levels were too low, and my doctor had to increase the prescribed thyroid hormones. Looking back at what happened, I know now that I had a flare-up: an autoimmune attack on the thyroid, but we didn't suspect it at this time.

In 2015 I was working for a smaller consulting firm. I remember that I started to feel unwell. My hair was falling out again by the handful, I felt an in-your-bones level of exhaustion, and my nails were brittle and breaking into the nailbed. I was also not sleeping, waking up at 2 o' clock in the morning and unable to fall asleep despite the feeling of exhaustion.

It was time to visit my doctor again. I phoned to make an appointment, but the receptionist told me that my doctor was on leave for the week. She offered to make an appointment with the locum doctor. I was desperate and I agreed to see her. This was without a doubt the best thing that could have happened to me.

The locum doctor was a tall lady with long red hair. She listened to my symptoms, and suggested we do blood tests to check the levels of the thyroid hormones, the iron levels, as well as the hormones oestrogen and testosterone. She then ticked the markers for the thyroid antibody tests as well. Two days later she received the blood test results back, and I was called in for an urgent consultation. Now, if you have ever been called into a doctor to discuss results, it is seldom to share any good news with you. I realized that something was very wrong. Sitting across from the doctor, she said that it looked like I had an autoimmune disease called Hashimoto's Thyroiditis. The doctor said she would like me to make an urgent appointment with a specialist physician to have a scan done to confirm the diagnosis.

Making an appointment with a specialist physician, as with any specialist, was a time challenge. Most of them only had an opening in three months and I could not wait that length in time.

After phoning around, I finally found a specialist physician that had an opening in two weeks. Arriving at the doctor's rooms at the scheduled time, the specialist physician did a thorough examination of the thyroid gland, followed by a sonar scan, and sat me down to explain the workings of the thyroid and the other female hormones. Is it not always interesting that while you are with the doctor everything makes so much sense, but once you leave, you cannot remember a thing? This is what happened to me. The only things I remembered were that he confirmed there were nodes on the thyroid, which was scarring tissue from the immune system attacking the thyroid gland, and that I did have Hashimoto's Thyroiditis. He also said that it was probably not cancerous, and that I had to eat more protein at breakfast.

Most people will turn to an internet search for information when they find out they have a medical condition. Needless to say, I did as well! I started reading about Hashi's, and within a few hours I was completely overwhelmed with the information. I did not know where to start, what to do, or what action I should take. It was too overwhelming. I just couldn't deal with it. So, I chose to ignore it all, with the exception of drinking my prescribed thyroid hormone replacement medication.

It was also in this year that the one thyroid medication that I was taking, Diotroxin, was discontinued by the pharmaceutical company. Diotroxin was a combination T4/T3 medication that I had been on for six years. I do believe that the discontinuation of this medication contributed to my thyroid frustrations.

A year passed, and I started getting really frustrated with feeling tired all the time. Another worry was the slow and steady pace at which I was growing out of my clothes! I had been picking up weight over the last 6 years, and I was becoming really worried and anxious about it. I made an appointment with my doctor, for the bi-annual check of the thyroid levels and asked her for advice. She suggested I make an appointment with an endocrinologist, and she provided me with the name and number of two endocrinologists. I managed to find an opening with one, however the wait would be two months.

This appointment was a disappointment. After an hour-long session, together with a sonar scan, a physical examination and a detailed questionnaire, he wrote a script and asked me to make follow-up appointment for six months' time. He was professional but he didn't listen to me. I wanted a more holistic approach to healing and for him, it was all about the medication. He didn't listen to my concerns as to what I was looking for, and just suggested more medication. I fired him.

By now it was 2018 and I had picked up a few more kilograms. I was very unhappy with my appearance, and the lack of ability to shake off the extra weight, regardless of exercise and eating healthy. In a conversation with a colleague about my concerns, she mentioned that if your hormones were not in-sync and at their optimal levels, you could do whatever you wanted but you would not be able to lose weight. She recommended I go and see her endocrinologist for a consultation. I made an appointment and waited three months to see him. When the time finally arrived, I was hopeful for an approach and advice that would help me feel better, and then to also lose weight. He listened to me, weighed me, and ordered an expensive series of blood tests. In the feedback consultation two weeks later (which also cost a huge amount money), he took me through the results and did a thorough explanation of the workings of the thyroid. By now I was understanding this little organ better. My iron levels were fine, female hormones were fine, but my adrenal function was depressed as my cortisol levels were too high. He also tested for Vitamin D and confirmed that the levels were insufficient. He slightly increased the thyroid medication, put me on a high dosage Vitamin D supplement, and some other supplements to support the adrenal functions. He suggested meditation and yoga as well.

I am telling you this story as it is not unique to me. Many other people who have been diagnosed with Hashi's have gone through a similar process of going from doctor to doctor to doctor in the hope of finding someone to help.

Six months later I went for the check-up blood tests, and in the consultation with the endocrinologist, he confirmed that the thyroid levels were at optimal levels, but I had added three kilograms to my weight. He said that I should have lost weight by now, and that I needed to go and see a dietician to help me with my eating habits. I was not impressed with his comments – did he really think I wanted to be overweight when I had been slim and energetic up to ten years ago? Anyway, he kept the thyroid medication at the level where it was and decreased the Vitamin D supplement. I asked him about the T3 hormone as an addition to my medication regime, but he said he rarely prescribed T3 hormones as he considered it a last resort.

I followed this regime for another six months. It was also during this this time that I experienced tremendous stress at work, and I wasn't sleeping well. Not sleeping well can really make you lose your mind! In 2019, I joined a South African Hashimoto's support group on Facebook and realized that many other Hashi's patients have had great results working with a functional doctor. Functional doctors don't just treat the symptoms, they focus on finding the underlying root cause and help you to heal. I decided it was time to visit a functional doctor, and I made an appointment for March 2019. I was pleasantly surprised with her. Again, she asked me to do blood tests, but her approach was very different to the other doctors. She started me with the additional T3 medication, increased my Vitamin D, added testosterone cream to my regime, added DHEA supplement, and recommended LDN (low dose Naltrexone). This was finally the start to my healing journey!

I had also started to adjust my eating habits, as well as other important lifestyle changes. I do believe these changes made a significant difference in getting my health and energy back. There were many changes I had to make, and a lot of work to do on what I understood to be healthy. Many things we have been told to be healthy, are not healthy at all when you have Hashimoto's Thyroiditis. Some of these beliefs have to be debunked in relation to Hashi's.

On Friday afternoon, 21 December 2019, my husband's company closed – it was sudden and unexpected. A series of decisions in the two months leading up to this date created a perfect storm, and everyone in the company received their retrenchment letters. I am sharing this with you because of the huge amount of stress that news like this creates! Stress is often a trigger for a Hashi's flare-up, and every time I have had a flare-up in the last 15 years since my underactive thyroid diagnosis, stress was involved in one way or the other. However, this time I didn't have a flare-up. This time I didn't collapse. I didn't experience any panic attacks, any decrease in energy or sleepless nights. I wasn't blind to what was happening, and I was clearheaded in my approach as to how we were going to deal with the situation.

What made the difference this time around? I believe it was the changes I made to my diet, my sleep routine, and having addressed nutrient deficiencies with the right supplements. This process made me realize that I had created the resilience in my mind and my body to weather this storm. I "coped". Well, truth be told, I was able to sail through this crisis with ease. This for me was proof that even though you cannot control many of the things that happen to you, you can take charge of your life and your response to these things. You can take charge of your environment, your food and your life, intelligently and with peace of mind.

BEING YOUR SOMEONE

At the time of writing this book, I am feeling great! You can do many things to improve your health, and the biggest test to know if something is working or not, is to simply ask one question: **how am I feeling?** It's not about whether the blood test results are in the normal range, it is about how you are feeling.

Over the last two years, I have researched and come to terms with Hashi's and what one can do to feel better. I remember the frustration and the overwhelming feeling when I received my diagnosis; the desperation for someone to guide and help me on what to do and when to do it. This is the reason why I have chosen to write this book: to help others make sense of what they can do, step by step, in a way that the information can be digested and give a feeling of empowerment through action.

If you have Hashimoto's Thyroiditis, this book is a practical guide on what you should know without an overload of medical jargon, what you should test for to understand your status and what you can do, step by step, to not just feel better, but to look better too.

I have learned that every person will experience Hashi's differently. I have learned it's just not enough to take your thyroid medication. I have learned that you must change your mindset, your lifestyle, remove toxins and always be kind to yourself. I have learned that what we have been taught are healthy foods, are the exact foods that keep us in a state of dis-ease. I have learned that healing is a journey, and on a journey such as this, it is easier if you do it with someone who knows and understands what you are going through.

This is what I believe my role is: to be your "someone", to help you make sense of what you need to know and to enable you with the tools and strategies that you can implement in your life to feel and look better.

My aim is to give you the motivation, the inspiration and the knowledge to live the life you were destined to live. You are not designed to be in dis-ease. You are meant to have the energy, focus and mental resilience to do the things you want to do, when you want to do it and to do it with vigor and passion. We should not just survive. We should thrive!

However, before we begin, I need to make it clear:

I AM NOT A DOCTOR

I am, however, a mom, wife and full-time professional who was diagnosed with an underactive thyroid in 2003, finally being diagnosed with Hashimoto's Thyroiditis after many years of struggling with debilitating symptoms.

During this time I have read many books about thyroid health and Hashimoto's Thyroiditis. I have seen many general physicians, specialist physicians, endocrinologists, homeopaths and dieticians in the hope of finding a solution – of feeling better and getting my energy back. With every doctor treating their area of focus, it has been many years of hoping to feel better, but not ever actually feeling like myself.

One of the biggest debilitating symptoms for me was the in-your-bones-feeling-like-death exhaustion. Even with sleeping nine to ten hours a night, I woke up wanting to go back to sleep because I just didn't have the energy to get up.

Every time I had a flare-up I experienced symptoms like hair loss, nails becoming brittle and breaking at the slightest bump, memory loss and brain fog, panic attacks and emotional to the point of crying one moment and deep and intense anger the next. This is not normal, and there were times that I was hoping it was something as simple as depression because then I could get help. However, it was the thyroid that went completely rogue that caused my health crisis.

It may be worth pointing out very early that if you feel a doctor would be qualified to advise you on the health of your thyroid, the average doctor will spend just a few hours in their entire six years of studies on the endocrine system and a few hours on autoimmune conditions and diseases. Most allopathic doctors will focus on treating the symptoms, and most specialists will focus on their area of speciality and treat within their area – either the immune system, or the thyroid gland. With Hashi's, it is far more than a thyroid disfunction problem. It is an immune system problem that has a major impact on the thyroid gland.

The rate at which autoimmune diseases are being diagnosed is increasing (and improving), and yet most of the medical profession still treat the symptoms and don't focus on finding the underlying cause of what is actually triggering the immune system in the first place. More and more medical professionals are now changing their approach from an allopathic perspective to a more holistic and functional perspective. There is an increase in awareness and more discussions and research on autoimmune diseases and how to help people back to health.

It is for this reason that I am hopeful, as well as excited! We are moving away from just popping more pills and shifting the focus to make the changes in our lives so that we can live long, happy, and healthy lives.

I AM NOT ANTI-DOCTOR OR ANTI-PHARMA

With treating hypothyroidism and Hashimoto's Thyroiditis, you will likely need synthetic thyroid hormones to replace the hormones that your thyroid cannot produce anymore. These medications are lifesaving, not just in terms of physical health, but also mental health. Thyroid hormone replacement therapy can help with many of the debilitating symptoms of an underactive thyroid. However, if the immune system is not calmed, over time the symptoms of thyroid dysfunction will vary between being overactive to being underactive as the immune system slowly continues to destroy the thyroid gland.

When a patient has an underactive thyroid, most doctors will not do the tests to check if the autoimmune disease Hashimoto's Thyroiditis, is causing the thyroid to be underactive. The reason, I believe, is that according to what they have learned in medical school, the treatment is the same: to prescribe thyroid hormones. So, the logic is why waste money on testing for thyroid antibodies when the treatment is the same? The problem is that you need to replace the thyroid hormones that your thyroid gland cannot produce anymore, as well as take action to calm the immune system and reduce inflammation. The process to health is more complex than simply taking some pills. It requires changes to your lifestyle, tweaking your diet, managing your stress and reducing toxins. Moreover, it is here where allopathic doctors typically are not able to help you.

Let me reiterate this: without my thyroid medication and other medication, Hashi's would have been debilitating for me. The thyroid medication is only the first step in many changes that you need to make in order to get your health back.

I AM NOT A SCIENTIST

There are a great many respected researchers and scientists who contribute to the growing knowledge of disease and treating disease. My approach is based on knowledge from scientists and researchers.

The approach and suggestions in this book are based on my experience, the experience reported by other Hashi's patients, and the research that is currently available. The problem is that

Hashimoto's Thyroiditis is different for every person, and it is for this reason that the experiences and lessons learned from other people who have Hashi's are also included in the research. Lastly,

I AM NOT A DIETICIAN OR NUTRIONIST

I haven't studied dietetics or nutrition at any university or other recognized institute. What I have learned about diet and nutrition is from conversations with dietitians and reading books on nutrition.

I also have had negative experiences with dietitians, when their education is only based on the old model of nutrition, where wholegrain and low GI wheat and dairy is at the core of what is considered a "healthy" diet. This out-of-date way of thinking may not be best for people who are striving to recover from an autoimmune disease. Just because it is taught by a respected and trusted institution such as a university, doesn't necessarily mean it is the best or right advice for you.

There are dieticians and nutritionists who challenge the status quo and who are the right people to have on your team. In later chapters of this book we will talk more about your team and who should be in your team to guide, support and assist you.

So, I am not a doctor, dietician, pharmacist, scientist, nutritionist or specialist. Then, who am I?

I AM YOU

I am a mom, wife, working professional, artist, speaker and photographer. I am a person with goals and dreams. I enjoy time with friends, exploring the outdoors, curling up to read a book and trying out new things. But, above all, I am living proof that you can live a great life. I am what you experience. I share your pain, frustration, and many of the symptoms that you may experience. I struggle every day with demands on my time and energy and having to fight the urge to get back into bed and stay there. I am, in fact, just like you.

I have written this book for you. If only someone had written a book like this for me, so that when I was first diagnosed, there would have been someone to guide me – firstly, by understanding Hashi's, secondly, by giving me information in an easy way so I could have had an informed discussion with my healthcare providers, and thirdly, a step-by-step plan to help me create the new habits and behaviors I needed to get back to a healthy "new" normal. A life where I have the energy, mental sharpness and health to live the life I want to live.

This is what I want for you – helping you to live the life you want to live.

MY REQUEST TO YOU

It is very tempting to just page to the what-you-need-to-do part, and let's be honest here, there is nothing I can do to stop you from doing that. I want to ask you to one key thing before you start implementing any changes:

READ THE BOOK

Please, read the book first. Please don't underestimate the importance of being fully aware and prepared to the make changes that you need in your life, the information that you need to understand and the strategies you need to take in order to claim your health back. Because here is the reality: you will have to change everything. EVERY SINGLE THING. In order to get your energy back, to feel better and become healthy, and in the process, lose some of the weight that you picked up due to Hashi's, you will have to make changes to every aspect to your life. That can be extremely daunting, and that is why I am here to help you – to guide you, to support you, and to motivate you. Change is scary, and the comfort zone is so very comfortable! This is why this book is here - to help you understand the changes that you need to make, why it is important that you do make them, and ultimately, give you a sustainable and happy way of living life.

Before we do that, I need to state the disclaimer and intended use of this book and any other material that I have already created, and may create in the future:

THE DISCLAIMER AND INTENDED USE OF THIS BOOK

This book is available to you as an information source about Hashimoto's Thyroiditis only. Any medical advice in this book is intended as general information to guide you and should not be used in any way to diagnose, treat, cure, or prevent, any disease. The goal of this book is to provide information, suggestions and protocols for nutritional support and health maintenance.

The information and recommendations outlined in this book are not here as a substitute for personalized medical advice. Always consult with a qualified and licensed medical health provider (general practitioner or physician, endocrinologist or other qualified health care provider). I, the author of this information, cannot be held liable for the information contained herein or any inadvertent errors or omissions of information. I have done my best to ensure that the information is accurate and up to date.

Do not make any changes to your medication without the express consent of your qualified and licensed medical health provider (your doctor). I am not rendering professional advice of any kind to you personally, but I am merely providing general education and information to you about wellness topics and Hashimoto's Thyroiditis.

This book is not to be used to diagnose, treat, cure, or prevent disease. It is only provided to you as informational guidance so that you can be better informed about your body and your health.

If you know or suspect that you may be pregnant or have any physical or medical condition, it is imperative that you seek the advice of your doctor prior to using the advice and/or suggestions provided in this book.

I, the author, am not responsible for any loss, injury, or damage that allegedly arises from any information published in this book and related social media sites. You are responsible for any actions you take regarding your medical care. I do not undertake any obligation or liability relating to the content of this book.

By continuing with this book, you agree and acknowledge that you have read the above and agree to continue with the book.

Now that is out of the way, let's continue the journey.

HOW THIS BOOK IS STRUCTURED

We are going back to school, learning a little about biology, science and psychology. It is what I believe you need to know to take ownership of your healing journey. With that in mind, this book is divided into four parts.

Part 1 focuses on obtaining an understanding about what it is that you want to achieve. "Being healthy again" is a rather vague statement and we'll spend some time on this to ensure you understand your goals. The reason for this is that we are resistant to making changes to the habits we've developed over the years. By understanding what it is that you really want and how your mind is programmed to sabotage your efforts, you will be able to more effectively put strategies in place to make the changes you need in your life to become healthy again.

Part 2 takes you through the biology of the thyroid gland. I wrote this book to give you knowledge about how your thyroid works within your body, without overwhelming you with medical jargon and terminology. Your thyroid leads the way when it comes to metabolism and energy, and works closely with your adrenal glands, your liver and your intestines. The thyroid receives its instructions from the brain, and we'll investigate and be able to understand these messages from the brain to the thyroid. When you know how your thyroid gland works, you can have an informed discussion with your healthcare professionals about how you feel and what you are experiencing.

Part 3 is about understanding the immune system, and how it can go wrong, causing the autoimmune disease Hashimoto's Thyroiditis. We'll explore the current thinking about what is causing autoimmune diseases, as well as the symptoms of Hashimoto's Thyroiditis. We'll also discuss the blood tests that you should discuss with your doctor to diagnose and manage Hashimoto's Thyroiditis.

In **Part 4** we look at the different areas of action to take your health back. There are nine pillars, each with its own recommendations and action steps. This section is the core of the book and will provide you with the detailed information on what you need to know to support your journey to reclaim your life.

Are you ready to take the first step? Then let's get started.

PART 1: WHAT DO YOU WANT?

"Accept what is, let go of what was, and have faith in what will be."
David Avocado Wolfe

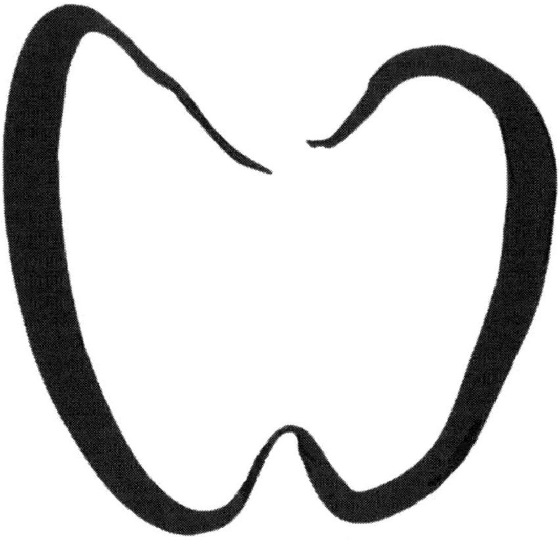

CHAPTER 1: BECOME VERY CLEAR ABOUT YOUR HEALTH GOALS

Imagine...

A year from today, you are looking back to this moment when you decided to reclaim your health. You look at the changes that you've made, and you're happy and proud with what you've achieved. You are feeling better, have regained energy that has been missing for so long, your mind is clear, and have even lost some weight. You are not just sleeping; you have a quality to your sleep that is rejuvenating! You have created new habits to support your health. You are enjoying healthy food that is life-giving. Your skin is glowing, your nails are growing, and your hair is luscious and strong. You have a lust for life, and you are doing things that you thought you'd never be able to do again. You are feeling good, no, let's rephrase that, you are feeling great! You are fabulous.

What do you want?

The above is an extract of the letter I wrote to myself. All except the first word "Imagine". These are the things that I wanted. Even though I can never be the same as before, I can redefine the new me. I want you to be able to do the same. I want you to know that you CAN be healthy and happy. You can have your energy back again. You can lose the weight that you may have picked up. You can have a clear mind again. You can have a healthy body even though you still have an autoimmune disease.

Is it possible to feel healthy again? Yes, I believe it is, as I am healthy again. And I am going to start the process by asking you this one question: What do you want?

It is such a simple question, but the answer you give is important. If your answer is "to be healthy again", I am going to ask you to go a little deeper. Why? Why do want to be healthy again? What would it mean to you? What would you want to do once you are healthy again? What are your dreams or goals that you have had to put on hold because of the symptoms of this autoimmune disease?

Write it down. Don't think too much about it. Just be real and honest with yourself. It is for you only, so you don't have to be flamboyant or fancy with your wording. Here are a couple of examples:

- I want to have energy at the end of the day to make dinner and play with my children.
- I want to be fit and run a marathon.
- I want to have my libido back so that my partner and I can be intimate again.

- I want to lose weight around my waist and butt, so I feel sexy again.

So, what do you really want? The clearer you are about what you want and why you want it, the easier it is going to be to commit to that decision. This part is important, and I don't want you to continue reading until you are clear about what you want to achieve. Write down your answers to these two questions on a piece of paper to keep:

What I really want is ______________________________.

The reasons why I want it are ______________________.

Your reasons are important, as they will be the fuel that will help you make the changes you need to make. Let's be honest, the things that are standing between you and what you really want, are your excuses, distractions, procrastination, and feelings.

Eliminate the resistance

Getting what you want is simple. However, it is not always easy. It is not easy because your brain does not like change. It prefers to work on autopilot, and whenever you want to make a change to anything, you will experience resistance. This resistance will come in the form of excuses, distractions, procrastination and feelings.

There are really only two words that can hinder your success: can't and won't. These two words are key to understanding what stands between you and your goal. The word "can't" is a euphemism for "won't": I cannot give up milk. I can't give up bread. I cannot find the time to exercise. I can't control myself around chocolate. You can say this for anything that you are struggling with, but let's be honest. The reality is that it is not that you cannot make the change, it is that you don't want to make the change. It is just an excuse. You don't believe me?

Do this exercise: for every statement that you believe you can't make a change, replace the word "can't" with the word "won't" and read these excuses again:

- I won't give up milk.
- I won't give up bread.
- I won't find the time to exercise.

This is powerful, right?

When you say you "can't" do it, it really means that you "won't" do it. Let's be honest - it is more truthful. You don't want to change. You don't feel like making the effort. It is scary and you don't know if you will have what it takes to make the changes and be able to stick with them. However, there is power when you take all your excuses and replace "can't" with "won't". First, it signifies that your excuse is not something that is out of your control, but that is a choice that you can make. Let's take a simple example of "I can't give up chocolate". By replacing "can't" with "won't", you take the power back: I won't give up chocolate. Herein lies the truth you must face: you don't want to make the change that you need to make, and you are hiding behind an excuse. You are not willing to put in the effort and the work. You are not willing to make the sacrifice that is required to get to your desired goal. And I know how hard it is. I have done it too!

The other forms of excuses are distractions and procrastination. Distractions include the things we do so that we can avoid what we need to do. I have had many distractions along my journey. Distractions include work, cleaning the house, working in the garden, starting a new project, watching a show someone said was unmissable, going out with friends, and even going on to social media to do "important" updates. These are all examples of distractions we use as a reason to avoid doing what we need to do.

Procrastination is another form of resistance, and it often 'walks together' with distractions. Have you ever said to yourself you will "start on Monday"? That is procrastination in its best form! Chocolate is one of my vices, and there was a time that I said to myself "today is the last time, tomorrow I'll be good, and I will not eat a chocolate". How many times do you think have I said this to myself? I'll be honest, more times that I care to admit to!

There is one more form of resistance that you will need to face head on, and that is that you are never going to feel like it. Change is hard, and when you wait for when you feel like it, it may never happen. You may never feel like doing the things you need to do, because it requires work and pushing yourself out of your comfort zone. Your brain doesn't like going out of the comfort zone. It loves living on autopilot. So, waiting until you feel like it, is not a good strategy to make changes. Because let's face it, you will never, ever, feel like it.

So, how do we get past the resistance? Let's explore this…

List your excuses

Look at the one thing that you want for your health. Next, write down all the possible excuses that you are likely to use to sabotage your efforts. The resistance will work hard to stop you from making the changes you need to make. We need to identify all these excuses and debunk them:

1. List 10 excuses or reasons that you are likely to use to stop yourself.
2. For each excuse, really look at it and write down the following: why this excuse is total nonsense (because it is nonsense!), and secondly, what are you are now willing to do instead – how will you eliminate the excuse, on a practical level.
3. Know that you will have to force yourself to make the changes. Accept that you will not feel like making the changes, and that it will be hard. Once you accept this reality, it will be easier for you to force yourself to make the changes you need to make to achieve your health goal.

There is one more issue that we will need to address before we start this journey. This may create conflict, frustration and confusion when we make the changes to our lives. What is it? It is the beliefs we have, and the stories we've been told, about food.

The stories we all were told and believed

There are stories that we all have heard that we need to investigate and then debunk. Here are a few of the stories that I was told while growing up:

1. The doctor knows best.
2. Fat is bad.
3. You need milk and yoghurt for calcium.
4. Low GI breads and pasta are better than high GI breads and pasta.
5. You can do anything as long as it is in moderation.
6. To lose weight, you need to burn more calories than you eat.
7. Just eat less and exercise more to lose weight.
8. Breakfast is the most important meal of the day.

These are just a random selection of the stories that I grew up with and believed. I had to debunk many of my beliefs around health and food. Sometimes I still remain stuck in old patterns and I find myself in an internal struggle between what I know now and what I have believed for a large part of my life.

What do you believe about health and food? What are some of the "facts" that you believe? What are the stories that you were told growing up? Take some time and write them down. Think about it over a day or two, as you prepare and enjoy your meals, exercise and work and just go about your day. Observe your beliefs and your reactions to your beliefs.

What is the story behind the stories we believe?

As you go through this content, you may find a resistance coming up when certain topics are being discussed. You may find yourself fighting with ideas, struggling to come to terms with them, and perhaps even outright challenging them. Remember it is part of your resistance. Resistance to change and resistance to being out of your comfort zone.

We are also being bombarded with health tips, tricks and information on every front. On social media the latest research and diets are openly promulgated and marketed, all to make money. Because let's face it: disease is money. The health industry is a big money-maker globally. People are looking for the next thing to help them feel healthier and look sexier and thinner.

The pharmaceutical industry is also big business. Sick people make them money and lots of it. I am not talking here of the emergency medical intervention needed to save a life. I am referring here to the "pill for every ill" phenomenon. For many people, when you feel ill, you go to the doctor to get a pill. It is almost like the easy way out of taking any accountability for your disease – just take a pill, and then I can still eat/drink/do what I want.

Now, let me make one thing very clear: with Hashimoto's Thyroiditis, a part or whole of your thyroid has been damaged and is not able to produce thyroid hormones. You need to take the thyroid hormone replacement therapy, because it really can save your life. Yet again, it is treating the symptom of an underactive thyroid, and not looking at why the immune system has gone awry to attack the thyroid gland tissues in the first place! In addition, even with taking the little white thyroid hormone replacement tablet, many people who have Hashi's still experience a range of debilitating symptoms. Because the real problem is inflammation!

What does this mean when you go to your doctor asking for help? Sadly, the experience of many people who have Hashi's, with allopathic doctors (including general practitioners, specialist physicians and endocrinologists) is that the doctors look only at the thyroid and optimizing the thyroid hormone replacement therapy. When you visit an immunologist, the immune system will then be under review, but the thyroid is not part of their expertise. When you see an endocrinologist, he or she will look at the endocrine system and the thyroid gland, but not at what needs to be done to calm the immune system.

This is why you will need to go on a journey to find a functional doctor (a medical doctor who has trained in functional medicine), who takes a holistic approach to your health, and not only treating the symptoms to make you feel better in the short term, but also to find the root cause of your immune attack.

I remember a time when I became so frustrated with my weight that I went to see a dietician. I explained that I had an autoimmune thyroid disease, and she still gave me an eating plan that included oats, rye bread and cottage cheese. As you will learn later, people who have Hashi's do well when they eliminate gluten and dairy.

Throughout this book, we'll be unpacking the stories that we have been told and what we need to change, not just in terms of beliefs and habits, but also in terms of how we go about life to give our bodies the best option to recover and heal.

Setbacks are also bound to happen. Let's pause here for a moment and talk about what to do when you have a setback.

Dealing with setbacks

Along your journey, you can, and most likely will, experience setbacks. A setback can be as simple as eating something that you shouldn't have, and you are experiencing some side effects, or as complicated as a full immune attack or flare-up. It's not a question of "if" it will happen, it's a question of "when" it will happen. I know it may sound a little negative, because we like to believe that once we make a decision, set a goal, create a plan and work the plan, it is a simple straight line from where we are now to the end state of being healthy, having energy and being at our best bodyweight. Regrettably life doesn't work that way. Your wellness journey is not going to be a straight line. Things will happen. What you need to have is a plan. More importantly, a plan that you can turn to so that when you have a setback, you don't just give up. A plan that allows you to have compassion for yourself.

Compassion for yourself is probably one the hardest things I had to learn. As a typical A-type personality, with the button always on and with there-is-always-something-to-do energy, taking time off to heal, rest and recover was, and still is, very difficult to do. I got frustrated and angry with my body for letting me down. I had to learn to care for myself. Compassion towards what you are going through is one of the key elements of recovery.

Just know that there will be bumps in the road. Do not despair. The thing to remember is that you are on a journey to health and this book is here to help you.

Now, forget the goal and focus on the process

Goals are great, really, they are. Goals are great for enabling you to focus on what you really want. They help to prioritize your energy and focus, as you simply do not have enough time in each day to do everything you want to do. You must make choices on what you want to focus on now, and what you are going to defer to later. This is why setting goals for your health are great! It will help you to focus on what you really what, and why it matters to you.

Let's talk about motivation and willpower. Motivation is essential to get you started! You decide to focus on something, that you are going to work hard to achieve that thing, and you experience that amazing jolt of energy and motivation. However, motivation is not enough to keep you going. Maybe you think you will rely on your willpower to keep you going each day. Unfortunately, research has shown that willpower is not reliable in helping you when things get tough, which inevitably, will happen. Willpower is a depleting resource. With every decision you make in the day, your willpower is used up little by little, and there may come a time in the day that your willpower is simply… gone! Here is a good example: you are going to start a diet to lose weight. You have seen the dietician, bought all the right foods, you are motivated and focused, and this time you are going to eat healthy fruits and vegetables, and avoid the chocolates, coffee and other comfort foods. Then, you have a challenging day at work. You feel tired and you are standing in the line at the supermarket, and the chocolate is calling your name. At first glance, you resist it, but then, even though you know you shouldn't, you buy the chocolate and eat it even before you get home. This has happened to me more times than I care to remember.

If your initial motivation and your willpower is not going to help you reach your goals, then what will help?

The answer lies in the process. The process, according to author Jeff Haydon in his book "The Motivation Myth", is what will help you achieve the success you want. Decide on your goal or goals, then design the process to help you get to you there. Then, Jeff says, forget about the goal and just focus on the process.

I want to take it a little further. In designing the process, you will also need to look at your routines and habits. You will need to look at the routines that you have in place and the habits that you do every day without even realizing what you are doing. You will have to make changes, and most of those changes will be to change what you normally do – your routines and habits.

You will also have to rethink what you believe. For example, breakfast. Who said that breakfast must be cereal and milk or bacon and eggs? You can have chicken and vegetables for breakfast! If you just had a reaction to having chicken and veggies for breakfast, that is a belief right there!

When you focus on creating a new process, you will inevitably change your routines, and you will focus on creating new habits.

Some habits will be easy to change, and some habits may always linger in the dark corners of your mind and will be hard to change.

Another word for process is "plan". Create a plan, and then the only thing you do, is adhere to the plan. With a plan, you remove the need to make a choice, and therefore you remove the reliance on your willpower. And you don't need any motivation, as the only thing you need to do is stick to the plan.

When looking at plans, routines and habits, there are many tips and strategies that we'll cover. One such tip, for example, is to have the same meal for breakfast and lunch and bring in variety with dinner.

There is one last thing I am going to ask you to do before we get into the content of this book. This exercise is simple, but the impact is huge. Every time you experience a setback, I want you to read what you have written to yourself, and the next part I'll show you exactly how.

Write a letter to your future self

I want you to imagine yourself a year from today. I want you to imagine how far you have come along your health journey. I want you to think about the changes that you have made, the things you have cut out from your life and the things you have introduced that brought you joy. I want you to think about how you are feeling today, and how you want to feel a year from today. Take some time and really explore the possibility of what your life could be a year from today.

Now, I want you to get paper and a pen. Don't type out your letter on a computer or on your phone or tablet. I want you to go old-school: writing with a pen on paper. It is now time to write that letter to yourself.

In this letter to yourself, put yourself in a time a year from now. Address the letter to yourself, and I want you to reflect on the positive changes you have made to get your health and energy back. Write about the dark moments when you felt overwhelmed and tired and hopeless, and how you have overcome those moments. Write about the day when you slipped, and what you did to get back on your plan, and lastly, write about how proud you are to have achieved what you wanted to achieve.

You may not yet know exactly what you need to change in your life, and I don't want this lack of information hold you back from writing your letter. You can still write the letter, even if you don't know the specifics of what you need to do. You know yourself, so you know what your stumbling blocks will be. For example, you may know that you don't like exercise, so in your letter you may write how you went to find some form of movement and exercise that you enjoy and how you have started to do this activity every week. Or, you know that chocolate is your weak point when you are stressed, and you can write how you are proud of yourself for finding other ways to deal with stress instead of reverting to chocolate.

Before you continue with this book, I want you to take the time to write this letter. Really. Do it now. I'll wait for you.

Write it now.

Have you written it? If you answer yes, then please continue reading. If you haven't written it, I am serious, please stop here and write this letter to yourself.

Now that you have written your letter, don't pack it away somewhere where you will forget about it. Put it somewhere where you can easily find it. Even better, put it in a space where you can see it every day, like on your refrigerator.

Now I just want to highlight one more important point: your body doesn't want to be ill. It wants to heal, so…

Give your body the best chance to heal

Your body wants to heal. This is your wake-up call. You have an autoimmune disease. There is no cure (yet). You have this for the rest of your life. It's your choice whether you are going to let this disease define you, or whether you are going to look at this as an opportunity to understand it and to make better choices.

Your body wants to heal. Give it the best opportunity to do just that.

The Five Golden Rules

There are five golden rules that I recommend you adopt and embrace. These are the lessons that I have learned the hard way from my own mistakes and from the experiences of other people with Hashi's.

Golden Rule Number 1: Knowledge Is Power

Learn about the thyroid, about the medications, about the latest research. When you know what is happening in your body, you have valuable information to discuss with your team of doctors and you can make informed decisions about what is working for you, and what is not working for you.

Golden Rule Number 2: You Are Your Best Advocate

You know your experience, your symptoms, your strengths and your limitations. Don't allow any doctor to tell you it's all in your head, that you will always feel tired and never lose the weight. Never allow any doctor or specialist to dismiss how you feel or what you experience. You are your own most important advocate in your healthcare.

Golden Rule Number 3: The Goldilocks Principle

The biggest frustration in the journey to feeling better is the process to find out what works for you. As you read about the experiences and lessons from other people who have Hashi's, you will find that some things will work for you, and some things just won't. It's like being Goldilocks in the fairy tale: you want to find the right porridge, the right chair and the right bed. We are all different and different things will work for different people. What might be right for one, may not be the right thing for you. The Goldilocks principle is about finding out what works for you.

Golden Rule Number 4: Keep it Simple

Do one very small change, so small that it is so simple to do that you cannot fail. In this plan, my aim is to make the action so small that it is easy to do and implement. Do this one thing for a few days, until it becomes part of "this-is-just-what-I-do". You can almost say, until it becomes a habit. Some of the actions will be easy, and some actions will take a little more effort and even more preparation. Don't be scared of the change. Small changes are small by design. Don't underestimate the impact of small changes that build on each other. Over time, all the small changes added over time make a big change in your life! I don't want to you to try and change everything overnight. Willpower and discipline are limited resources, and when they run out, you will go back to your old ways – that is the power of habits! We want to avoid that from happening! However, if you do fall off the bandwagon, for whatever reason....

Golden Rule Number 5: Catch that Wagon

If you eat gluten, if you used toothpaste with fluoride, if you are going through a tough time at work and are stressed, don't throw your hands in the air and scream that it was "all for nothing" and now you are going to binge on chocolate chip cookies! A little dramatic, I know. The point is that you are, after all, human. This is a journey. If you fall off the wagon, don't beat yourself up over it. What I do want you to do, is to catch the wagon and get back on! Take a breath, calm down, and just go back to doing what you were doing before. You are doing great, keep making small changes, one step at a time.

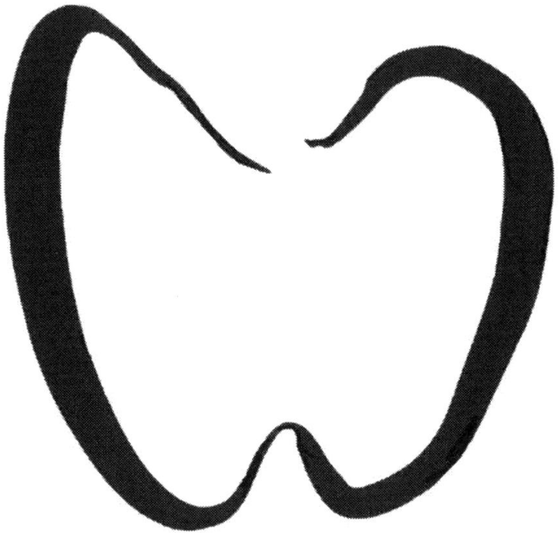

PART 2: YOUR THYROID - THE ENGINE OF YOUR BODY

"A lack of knowledge creates fear. Seeking knowledge creates courage."
Candice Swanepoel

CHAPTER 2: HOW YOUR THYROID WORKS FOR YOU

You must know your own biology. Knowing how the thyroid works is the first step in your journey to reclaim your life. When you need to go for blood tests, you need to know which blood tests to ask for. When recommendations are made for medication, you want to be in a position of knowing how this it will impact your body. So, let's start by looking at the thyroid gland and what the function of the thyroid gland in the body is.

The thyroid gland is a butterfly-shaped organ that is based in the lower part of your neck. It is a gland (also called an endocrine as it is part of the endocrine system) as it releases hormones into your body. These hormones play a critical part in multiple functions in your body, including metabolism, body temperature, blood pressure, heart rate, nerve function, growth, development, and clear thinking.

Knowing how your thyroid is supposed to work will help you when things do not work as they are supposed to. And let's be honest, when your thyroid is having a bad day, it can affect your entire life.

The key role of the thyroid

The thyroid gland has one main function in the body: to produce the thyroid hormones that are used by every other cell in the body for energy. The thyroid hormones are then secreted into your blood stream to be delivered to the cells in your body. The two main thyroid hormones are T4 and T3 hormones.

The process of making these thyroid hormones is important to know. The thyroid gland takes iodine from your food and combines it with an amino acid called tyrosine (which is also produced by the thyroid gland) to make the thyroid hormones. The thyroid gland combines the tyrosine and iodine to make the thyroid hormones:

- Thyroxine, known as T4, as it has four iodine molecules,
- Triiodothyronine, known as T3, as it as three iodine molecules.

However, these two hormones are not made in equal quantities. The thyroid gland makes mostly T4 and only a little T3. It is estimated that about 94% of the hormones created by the thyroid are the T4 hormone, and the remaining 6% is the T3 hormone.

There is an important difference between these two hormones. The T3 hormone is the active hormone that the cells can use for metabolism and other functions, while the T4 is the inactive form. The body must convert T4 into T3 before it can be used.

The conversion of the inactive T4 hormone to the active and available T3 hormone occurs in a few areas in the body: the liver, gut, heart, muscles, and nerves. Most of the conversion occurs in the liver.

But not all the T4 hormones are converted to T3 hormones. It is estimated that only about 60% of the T4 is converted to T3 in the liver, while about 20% is converted to T3 by healthy bacteria in the digestive tract. The last twenty percent becomes Reverse T3 (rT3), which the body cannot use.

Transporting the thyroid hormones

The blood transports the thyroid hormones to the cells by binding the thyroid hormones to a protein called TBG (Thyroid Binding Globulin). When the thyroid hormone takes a ride with TBG, it cannot be used by the cells, during which they are called "bound". When the thyroid hormones are delivered for duty, they are called "free" hormones and available for use.

A balancing act

Thyroid hormones need to be just right for the body to work optimally, so there is a constant balancing act happening. The hypothalamus is part of the brain and monitors the levels of the thyroid hormones. When the levels of thyroid hormone are too low, the hypothalamus responds by releasing TRH (TSH Releasing Hormone), which goes straight to the pituitary gland. The pituitary gland is another member of the endocrine system and is also found in the brain. The pituitary gland's function is to produce a hormone called Thyroid Stimulating Hormone (TSH), which then instructs the thyroid to make more thyroid hormones and to release them in the blood for cells to use.

When the thyroid hormones are too high in the blood stream, the hypothalamus decreases the TRH hormone, which in turn instructs the pituitary gland to decrease its TSH production so that the thyroid gland produces fewer thyroid hormones.

The three glands work together to regulate the production and release of T4 and T3.

What could go wrong? Quite a lot it seems, and we'll go into that in the next section.

CHAPTER 3: WHEN THE THYROID MALFUNCTIONS

When the thyroid gland doesn't function as it is supposed to, it can cause a range of debilitating symptoms. When you have too few thyroid hormones in your body, the thyroid is underactive or hypothyroid, and when the thyroid produces too many thyroid hormones, the thyroid is overactive or hyperthyroid. Both overactive and underactive thyroid function have debilitating symptoms:

- **Underactive thyroid symptoms:** fatigue, cold intolerance, appetite loss, weight gain, high blood pressure and elevated levels of total and LDL cholesterol, difficulties with concentration, memory loss issues, lack of interest in important things that are normally important to you, dry skin, brittle nails, constipation due to slower digestive processes, heavier periods for women or even periods stopping, muscle aches and pains, or even balance problems in older women.

- **Overactive thyroid symptoms**: nervousness, palpitations caused by a faster heart rate, feeling hot when others are comfortable, trouble with sleeping, persistent tiredness and weakness, swelling in your neck from an enlarged thyroid gland (called a goitre) and weigh loss despite feeling hungry all the time. It can also lead to lower diastolic blood pressure as the blood vessels relax (the diastolic blood pressure is the bottom number in the blood pressure reading) and higher systolic pressure because of the increase in the force of the heart's contractions (the top number in the blood pressure reading).

There are several reasons why the thyroid can become under-active or over-active, or where any part of the chain above can break and lead to this situation. Let's have a look at where breakdowns may occur.

1. **Pituitary gland dysfunction**

   The pituitary gland is located in the brain, and is responsible for managing a range of hormones. There are several reasons why the pituitary gland may not function as well as it should. The pituitary gland is responsible for sending the hormone TSH (thyroid stimulating hormone) to the thyroid. If the pituitary gland is not working well, TSH to the thyroid might be impacted, and the thyroid doesn't produce enough T4 and T3.

   There are a few things that can impact the function of the pituitary gland function, including infection, blood sugar imbalances, chronic stress, pregnancy, hypoglycemia, or insulin resistance.

2. **Your body can't convert T4 to T3**

Your body needs to convert T4 to T3 for the cells to be able to use it. You may have enough hormones, but it is not being made available to the cells. This is technically not a thyroid gland problem, but a problem elsewhere in the body that is affecting the thyroid system. There are several reasons why this may occur, such as inflammation, high cortisol levels, a sluggish liver or liver disease, high oestrogen levels, heavy metal toxicity, aging, diabetes, surgery, radiation, or too little healthy gut bacteria.

3. **Too little or too much TBG in your blood**

Thyroid hormones hitch a ride on the protein TBG (thyroid binding globulin) in your blood, and while the thyroid hormones are attached to TBG, it's not available to the cells. When TBG is too high or too low, it can cause problems:

- TBG can be elevated due to high oestrogen levels, which are often associated with birth control pills or oestrogen replacement. With high levels of TBG, the levels of free thyroid hormones will be low. Elevated oestrogen creates too many TBG's (thyroid binding globulin) so to that the thyroid hormones cannot get into the cells
- TBG can be low due to high testosterone levels. In women, this is commonly associated with PCOS and insulin resistance. With low TBG, the levels of free thyroid hormones will be high, which is good, right? Unfortunately, not. Too many free

thyroid hormones can cause the cells to develop resistance to the hormones, and then the cells can't use them.

4. **The immune system**

   The body's immune system produces antibodies to attack foreign invaders and to fight off viruses and bacteria. With inflammation, the antibodies then also attack a part of the body in a case of mistaken identity, causing what is called an autoimmune reaction. Hashimoto's Thyroiditis is a situation in which the immune system is attacking the thyroid gland, and over time, the thyroid cells are damaged and not able to produce thyroid hormones any longer.

5. **Hyperthyroidism or Grave's Disease**

   It is strange to think that a case of overactive thyroid can lead to an underactive thyroid. People who have too high a level of thyroid hormone (called hyperthyroidism) are often treated with radioactive iodine or anti-thyroid medication to limit the production of thyroid hormones. Sometimes these treatments can lead to lowering the thyroid production too much, resulting in permanent hypothyroidism.

6. **Removal of the thyroid gland**

   Removing a part of the thyroid gland can reduce thyroid hormone production, and in some cases removal of the thyroid gland is required, which will leave a need to replace all the thyroid hormones with medical treatment.

7. **Medications and certain therapies**

   Certain medications can lead to an underactive thyroid, for example lithium (used to treat certain psychiatric disorders). Radiation and chemotherapy to treat certain cancers can impact the ability of the thyroid gland to produce thyroid hormones.

8. **Pregnancy**

   Some women can develop hypothyroidism during or after pregnancy. This can be a problem, as hypothyroidism in pregnancy can increase the risk of miscarriage, premature delivery and preeclampsia (characterized by higher blood pressure in the last three months of pregnancy). It can also impact the development of the fetus.

9. **Iodine deficiency**

   Iodine is a trace mineral that is found in iodized salt, seafood, seaweed, and plants that grow in iodine-rich soil. Although iodine is needed by the thyroid to make the thyroid hormones, there can be a problem in that there is too little iodine available in the body. The thyroid therefore cannot produce the thyroid hormones. Supplementing with iodine is a controversial topic in the medical world, and we'll talk more about it later.

When you have Hashi's, it is not really the thyroid that is malfunctioning. It is the immune system that is going on full alert and into attack mode for what can be one or more of many reasons, and your thyroid gland is under fire from the immune system. Thyroid tissue is destroyed, and you become hypothyroid (underactive) over time, with bouts of hyperthyroid (overactive) when your immune system attacks the thyroid gland!

Next, we are going to look at the immune system and how it impacts our bodies.

PART 3: YOUR IMMUNE SYSTEM AND HASHI'S

"You can either say you are going through something or you can say you are growing through something."
Jewel (singer/songwriter)

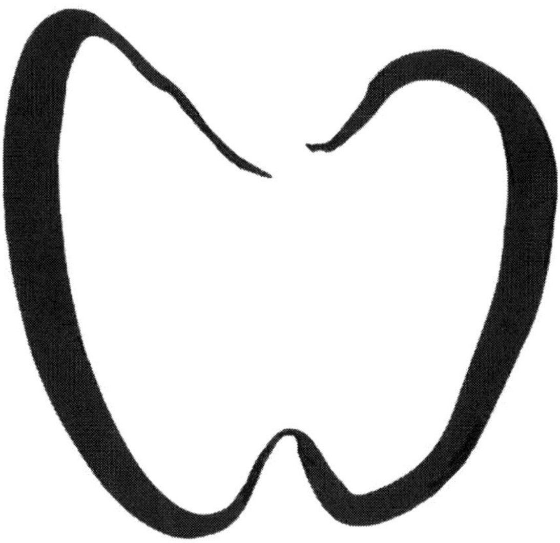

CHAPTER 4: AN AUTOIMMUNE DISEASE THAT AFFECTS THE THYROID FUNCTION

Many people who have been diagnosed with an underactive thyroid gland are never tested for thyroid antibodies. It is estimated that about 60% of underactive thyroid patients have Hashimoto's Thyroiditis, but because doctors are not looking for what is causing the underactive thyroid, most people who struggle with Hashi's are not diagnosed.

When I look back on my experience with the various doctors I consulted, I know now that I probably already had Hashi's by the time I was diagnosed with an underactive thyroid in 2003. I struggled for many years with symptoms shifting between under and overactive thyroid – because of flare-ups. I know that my thyroid gland has been damaged to such an extent that I will need to take thyroid hormones for the rest of my life. I also know now that I must address my immune system to stop the attack on my thyroid gland. I must save and protect what is left of my thyroid gland.

Let's now get a better understanding of what exactly Hashimoto's Thyroiditis is.

What is Hashimoto's Thyroiditis?

Hashimoto's Thyroiditis is an autoimmune disease where the immune system is attacking the thyroid gland. So over time, the immune system destroys thyroid cells, and your thyroid gland becomes underactive (hypothyroid) as it cannot produce the number of thyroid hormones that the body needs anymore.

When the immune system attacks the thyroid gland, the damaged thyroid cells release thyroid hormones into the bloodstream leading to a surge of thyroid hormones. This can lead to a period of hyperthyroidism – when there are too many thyroid hormones in your body. When this happens, you can experience overactive thyroid symptoms, like a racing and pounding heart and anxiety. But this is only a temporary increase!

As your body adjusts to the surge in thyroid hormones, the pituitary gland in the brain instructs the thyroid gland to make fewer thyroid hormones, and the level of thyroid production is lowered. Once the level of hormones stabilizes, the impact of the damaged cells is clear: they cannot produce thyroid hormones anymore, and so the thyroid produces fewer hormones from now on.

But the story doesn't stop there. The body needs a certain level of hormones that the thyroid gland just cannot produce anymore. It's like the body is screaming at the pituitary gland to tell the thyroid to make more thyroid hormones, but regardless of the increased instructions to the thyroid gland (a high TSH level), the thyroid just isn't able to make the much-needed thyroid hormones. Over time, as you have flare-ups in your immune system and attacks on your thyroid, your thyroid will become less and less effective. As the autoimmune disease progresses, you get to a state of chronic thyroid hormone underproduction.

While doctors still don't really know what causes autoimmunity, the best theory is that autoimmunity is a case of mistaken identity. Here's how it works: something happens or something enters into the bloodstream and the immune system is activated. As part of the immune system's defense mechanisms, it activates antibodies. The job of the antibodies is to neutralize and destroy the pathogens. The problem is that the structure of the pathogens looks very similar to the structure of the thyroid gland tissue, and the antibodies cannot distinguish between what is pathogen and what is the thyroid gland. The antibodies neutralize and destroy both the pathogens and the cells of the thyroid gland.

I have had immune system flare-ups over the years, and now I know it was my immune system doing its work to remove pathogens, and the thyroid gland was damaged in the process. Would it have helped if I was diagnosed earlier with Hashimoto's Thyroiditis? Perhaps. But I don't worry too much about that – what's done is done and I must look forward on how to prevent further flare-ups. Why? I don't want to increase my likelihood of developing other autoimmune diseases. It is believed that when you have one autoimmune disease, the likelihood of developing other autoimmune diseases increases. The theory is that the immune system can start to attack other parts of the body as well, like other glands, muscles, nerves, blood and even the skin! Calming the immune system attack is not just about helping you to feel better, it is also about helping to prevent the development of other autoimmune diseases.

Symptoms of Hashimoto's Thyroiditis

There are a wide range of symptoms that you may experience when you are having a Hashi's autoimmune flare-up. More importantly, the experience of symptoms may vary from person to person. You may experience both physiological symptoms (the body) and the psychological symptoms (the mind).

Let's start with the physiological symptoms that you may experience:

- Fatigue
- Lethargy
- Dry skin, eyes, mouth, or scalp
- Hair loss
- Sensitivity to cold
- Muscle and joint aches and pains
- Constipation
- Weight gain and/or difficulty losing weight
- Slowed metabolism
- Hoarseness or deepening of the voice
- Strangling or tight sensation in the throat

- Heavy or prolonged menstruation
- Enlarged thyroid (also called goitre)
- Problems with your appetite
- Struggling to sleep
- Episodes of excessive perspiring
- Rapid heart rate and heart palpitations

You may also experience some of the psychological symptoms:

- Brain fog and poor short-term memory
- Lack of concentration
- Loss of interest and ambition
- Anxiety and tension
- Emotional mood swings
- Impatience and being irritable
- Bouts of depression with sadness

When you are suddenly not feeling like yourself, you may be experiencing an autoimmune flare-up. You may also feel that you are losing your mind! When I become very emotional and my mood swings between anger, frustration, sadness and hopelessness, I know that I am likely experiencing an autoimmune flare-up and that there are too many thyroid hormones in my blood stream! It is scary to experience this. You are not losing your mind! It's your thyroid hormones that are on a rampage! Can you fix it? Yes, it is possible. Once you know what caused your immune system to trigger, you can take action to address it.

Five Stages of Hashimoto's Thyroiditis

Hashimoto's Thyroiditis doesn't just happen overnight. The autoimmune disease progresses over time, and it usually starts quietly, long before you feel ill or are diagnosed, and it can develop over many years. Research done by Wiersinga and colleagues (2014) identified five stages of Hashimoto's Thyroiditis:

Stage 1: Genetic predisposition

You have the genes that make you predisposed for Hashi's. You are not experiencing any of the symptoms of over- or under-active thyroid. You don't have Hashi's or experience any hypothyroid functions.

Stage 2: Immune cell infiltration of the thyroid gland

You start to develop immune activity (for many reasons) which attacks the thyroid gland in a case of mistaken identity. You start experiencing symptoms which impact your life, and it can be either hyperthyroid symptoms, followed by hypothyroid symptoms, or both. You might also experience digestive problems, fatigue, hair loss, or even sensitivity to cold. It is very likely that while you are in this stage, your thyroid blood tests will still show normal, as it can take years of gradual damage before the lab markers in blood tests will show results outside of the normal ranges.

Stage 3: Subclinical hypothyroidism

This is the stage where the immune system is working so well that there is now damage to the thyroid gland - the beginning of thyroid gland failure. The thyroid gland cannot produce enough T4 and T3 hormone anymore, and now it will show in your blood test results. The TSH will be elevated, as the body is asking the pituitary gland for more thyroid hormones, and the pituitary gland is giving more and more instructions, but the thyroid gland just cannot make the right number of thyroid hormones. At this stage your doctor will recommend that you take thyroid hormone medication. The common approach is to prescribe only synthetic T4 hormones, levothyroxine, to replace the T4 hormones that the thyroid gland cannot produce anymore.

Stage 4: Overt hypothyroidism

This is the stage where patients are usually diagnosed with Hashi's, as lab markers will be abnormal. There will be damage to the thyroid gland to the extent that the thyroid cannot produce the number of thyroid hormones that the body requires, and patients will need to take thyroid hormone medication to prevent serious health consequences. At this stage it is vital to take proactive action to address the immune system flare-up and to reduce the attack on the thyroid gland.

Stage 5: Progression to other autoimmune disorders

When patients don't make the necessary changes to their lives to calm their immune system, there is a risk that other autoimmune diseases will develop. Even if you take your thyroid medication and your lab markers for thyroid function are all "normal", you can still develop other autoimmune diseases. There are more than 80 types of autoimmune diseases as listed by Johns Hopkins Medicine. It is therefore important to monitor your health, and when you suspect that you may have another autoimmune disease (especially if the symptoms do not improve), to ask your doctor to test for other immune markers as well.

Why is it important to understand the stages of autoimmune disease development? Most people will only be diagnosed with Hashi's when they reach stage 4, or even at stage 5 when they have been developing other autoimmune diseases as well. The conventional treatment of prescribing thyroid hormones is like putting a plaster on a bullet wound. The immune system will continue to destroy thyroid gland cells until you find the root cause of what triggered the immune system and address that. Just taking thyroid hormone replacement therapy will not heal you. You must take ownership of your body and your health and make changes to your life to heal.

Are your genes to blame?

Why is it that some people will develop an autoimmune disease and others not? There are three factors that determine your predisposition to developing Hashimoto's Thyroiditis:

1. Genetic predisposition
2. What the thyroid gland absorbs
3. Your immune system

Let's have a quick look at each of these factors.

Factor 1: Genetic predisposition

Unfortunately, you cannot do anything about changing your genes (yet… but with the advances in medical science, who knows what the future may bring). Your genes may also make you more susceptible to developing an autoimmune disease.

There is an emerging science called epigenetics, which researches the phenomenon of the environment directly impacting the genes. It literally means "above the genes". The research done by Sir Adrian Bird, Dr Bruce Lipton and others is looking at how the environment can turn genes on or off. Turn genes on or off? Yes! In a very, very simplified explanation, the DNA in your cells is like the instruction manual for how the cell creates various functional proteins. Epigenetics affects how the cells read this instruction manual, the DNA. So certain things in your environment, for example the food that you eat, where you live, how you exercise, and even when you sleep, can cause chemical changes around the DNA, which can turn those genes on or off over time.

So, you have the genes that you have been born with, but your environment plays a very important role in your health. The choices you make, that make up your lifestyle, can impact the quality of your life.

Factor 2: What the thyroid gland absorbs

The second component that determines your likelihood to develop Hashi's is what the thyroid gland absorbs. The thyroid uses iodine to make thyroid hormones and it gets this iodine from food sources.

The problem is that there are other chemicals that have a similar structure to iodine, and the thyroid gland absorbs these chemicals as well. It looks similar to iodine, but it is not iodine. Some of these chemicals include mercury, which is found in high fructose corn syrup and dental amalgam fillings, cadmium from second-hand smoke, herbicides and pesticides used in crops and even the plastic homeware we use in our kitchens!

What is frightening is that there are approximately 300 chemicals which have been identified to be absorbed by the thyroid. This builds up in the thyroid, and the more susceptible you are (your genes), the quicker your thyroid will react.

Factor 3: Your immune system

The third component is your immune system. Your immune system is the protection system for your body, and it goes into attack mode when there is a threat. Now that your thyroid has '*weird stuff*' in it – it is inflamed, it is releasing free radicals in the body (which are corrosive and damaging to the body's cells), and so the immune system reacts by attacking the chemicals, and the thyroid gland becomes collateral damage in the process.

Now, we can't do anything about your genes. That is not in your control as you are stuck with what you have received from your biological parents. However, you can influence and control just about everything else in your body, as well as the things that cause the immune system to attack the thyroid gland. What is in your control? First, the chemicals that enter your body (through your food, your skincare and other environmental factors) and second, the actions you take to positively improve your immune system, including sleep and stress management. So even if you cannot do anything about your genes, you CAN control everything else!

Fix the Immune System, not the Thyroid

With Hashimoto's Thyroiditis, it is the immune system that is attacking the thyroid. While we need to look at the thyroid and replace the hormones with the right level of thyroid hormone medication, we also need to look at the immune system in relation to the thyroid function.

How the immune system works

Your immune system works hard to protect you from unwanted disease-causing germs (like bacteria, viruses, fungi and parasites), neutralizes harmful substances and pathogens from the environment and fights against disease-causing changes in the body (such as cancer cells). It works by either destroying the disease-causing pathogens or by filtering the blood and removing toxins from the body.

The immune system has cells to do the work, which are known as the T-helper cells, or Th cells, and these cells are part of the white blood cells that recognize pathogens. There are two very different subsystems of T-helper cells. They do different jobs yet work closely together:

- **Th1 system** is called the *innate or non-specific immune system*, and this is the body's first defense against harmful germs and substances. It uses immune cells such as natural killer cells to find harmful substances that enter the body. It causes inflammation and this system has been found to be involved in the development of organ-specific autoimmune diseases.
- **Th2 system** is called the *adaptive or specific immune system*, which creates antibodies and uses them to specifically fight certain germs that the body has previously encountered, like bacteria, toxins and allergens. This system tends not to be inflammatory, and it has been found to be involved in systemic autoimmune diseases and other chronic conditions.

If you research the immune system and autoimmunity online, you will find many references to the words Th1 dominance and Th2 dominance and that you should act based on whether you are Th1 or Th2 dominant. Before you act, let's take a moment to understand what exactly this is all about.

There is a theory about the balance between the Th1/Th2 systems, which led to the generally accepted belief that you could be Th1 or Th2 dominant. But it is a theory and limited studies have been done to date. The theory arose from a 1986 study that looked at the T-helper cells of mice, and how the T-helper cells have different patterns of communication and movement. This theory was then adapted to human immunity – which is now referred to as the Th1 and Th2 responses. The belief is that over-activation of either response can cause disease and can down regulate the other response. The hypothesis was tested, and it was found that the human responses rarely fell into exclusive Th1 or Th2 patterns. Some people claim that being Th1 or Th2 dominant might affect how you approach your healing journey. But there just isn't enough clinical evidence and research yet to verify the theory.

Limited studies have found that people with Hashimoto's Thyroiditis are Th1 dominant. But other studies have found that bacterial and viral infections activate the Th1 system, and at different points both the Th1 and Th2 systems were used to get rid of the invader! Then, the impact of how food affects the Th2 system is still unknown. To add to the confusion, the Th1 system is considered inflammatory and the Th2 system anti-inflammatory, yet evidence does not agree! Many allergic diseases have been likened with Th2 activity, while several auto-immune diseases have shown mixed Th1/Th2 responses. So, it is possible to have both elevated Th1 and Th2 activity!

I am sharing this with you as there are some practitioners that recommend testing for Th1 or Th2 dominance, and base their recommendations and prescriptions on this information, including what supplements to take and foods to eat and avoid. Be careful, as it is easy to accidentally stimulate the dominant response, which may cause the autoimmune attack to worsen. While it may be interesting to find out if you are Th1 or Th2 dominant, it may not be the best or safest approach as a way of treatment. A safer way is to focus on the things that help calm the immune system and not just focus on the Th1 or Th2 system.

Next, let's understand what the underlying causes are that can trigger the immune system.

Root causes of inflammation

While there are many reasons for a thyroid to malfunction, in the case of Hashimoto's Thyroiditis it is the immune system that has a case of mistaken identity - confusing the healthy thyroid cells with the invading pathogens.

Conventional medicine will focus on replacing the lacking thyroid hormones with pills that contain thyroid hormones, which I call thyroid hormone replacement therapy. Taking additional thyroid hormones is vital for your health, but with Hashi's, it is like putting a plaster on a bullet wound. Thyroid hormone replacement therapy (or thyroid medication as most people call it) does not address the immune system that attacks and damages the thyroid gland.

If we do not address the immune system, it will just keep on attacking the thyroid. The thyroid's function will continue to deteriorate over time, and you will need to take more and more thyroid hormones. There are experts who have done research based on observed feedback as well as their own approaches, based on functional medicine, who believe there are five underlying causes of autoimmunity. You can help the immune system by addressing these root causes, lowering the antibodies, and thereby reducing the symptoms of an underactive thyroid and feeling better. Isn't that what we want?

The five underlying causes of autoimmunity are:

1. Stress
2. Leaky gut
3. Gluten
4. Toxins
5. Infections

Stress

Stress has been shown to trigger and intensify autoimmune disorders. The research is not strong on the fact that stress causes autoimmune diseases, but stress is a huge contributor to flare-ups once you have an autoimmune disease.

Leaky gut

Leaky what? Yes, you have read it right: leaky gut, also known as intestinal permeability. It is a term used to describe what is happening in your gut. When you eat or drink food, it ends up in your digestive tract, where it is broken down into nutrients so that it can be absorbed into the blood stream. The wall of the gut filters nutrients into the bloodstream, and blocks larger elements, like toxins and pathogens, from entering the bloodstream. With leaky gut, the gaps in the gut wall don't close, and the larger elements enter the bloodstream. The immune system reacts to these toxins and chemicals that are not supposed to be there, and goes into action to attack and remove these pathogens and toxins from the body.

Gluten

Gluten is a protein found in wheat and other grains. If you have an autoimmune disease, the first thing you are recommended to do is to remove gluten from your diet and from your environment. There are three reasons why gluten should be avoided:

- **Gluten causes leaky gut.** Gluten triggers the release zonulin in the gut which opens the little gaps in gut wall, therefore creating leaky gut (from the research done by Dr Alessio Fasano).
- **Gluten causes inflammation**. The gluten goes through the gut wall into the blood, and the immune system goes to work to get rid of the unwelcome element, leading to the inflammation response. And this leads to the next point:
- **Gluten looks like your own healthy tissue**, the thyroid tissue. As the immune system is attacking the unwanted elements in the blood by creating antibodies, it also attacks the thyroid gland. Every time you eat gluten, the immune system sends out antibodies to detect and destroy gluten, and by mistaken identity, the thyroid gland tissue is also attacked and destroyed.

Toxins

Toxins in our bodies and environment can trigger the immune system. Toxins are everywhere, including our cleaning products, personal care products, mold, pollution in the air and water, and even in amalgam dental fillings.

Infections

Scientists have suspected that infections from bacteria, viruses and parasites can cause autoimmunity. In fact, there are several infections that have been linked to autoimmunity already, in being a trigger or worsening symptoms, here are a few:

- Epstein Barr virus (which causes mono) has been strongly correlated with multiple sclerosis (MS), chronic fatigue syndrome (CFS), lupus and Grave's Disease.
- E.coli
- Herpes Simplex 1 and 2 (gives you cold sores and/or genital herpes)
- Lyme disease caused by a bacteria
- Human parvovirus
- Blastocystis hominis
- Mumps
- Rubella
- Sinus infections
- SIBO (small intestinal bacterial overgrowth)
- Hepatitis C

Infections can hide just about anywhere in the body, including your thyroid gland. One of the problems that some pathogens have is that they have a similar structure to the cells of the thyroid gland, while others can infect the thyroid gland. Many infections can also cause leaky gut.

Now that we know what the underlying root causes of inflammation are, we can take action to fix it. Ready? Let's go!

PART 4: TAKING YOUR HEALTH BACK

"Start by doing what's necessary; then do what's possible; and suddenly you are doing the impossible."

Francis of Assisi

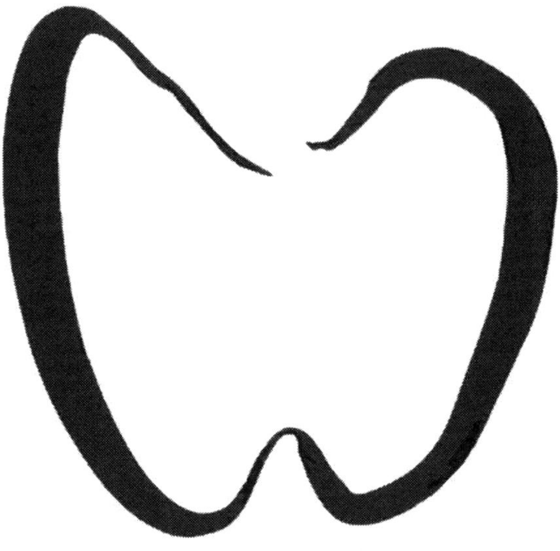

CHAPTER 5: THE NINE PILLARS OF HASHIMOTO'S HEALTH

Now is the time to understand what we can do to feel better, get our energy back and live the life that we want. Hashimoto's Thyroiditis is an autoimmune disease which you will likely have for the rest of your life, but it doesn't mean it should ruin or define your life. I believe that the approach is multi-faceted, like a puzzle, and each piece of the puzzle is needed. Food and eating healing foods are a large component of calming the immune system, but is not the only piece of the puzzle. There is much more that you can, and should, do.

You may be tempted to want to just jump in and change everything on the first day, but I want to ask you to not do that. Don't change everything all at once. We want to focus on creating lifestyle changes that can be easily incorporated into our lives. While we do need to change everything, we don't need to change everything at the same time.

If you are like me, too much change can be overwhelming. It is because our brains don't like change. One of the reasons why making change can be so hard is if the change is too big. When we break down any change into its smallest component, it makes it easier to do and to keep on doing it. Over time, small changes done regularly become new habits. Once it is a habit, it is easy to keep it going.

More importantly though, give your body the best chance to heal itself. I believe that the body can heal itself, and we must do the right things to help the body to heal itself. Therefore, I believe we need to focus on the following outcomes:

1. Optimize the thyroid hormones for what your body needs to function at its best.
2. Manage your stress to reduce the long-term impact of cortisol and adrenaline in your body.
3. Heal leaky gut.
4. Identify and remove foods that can trigger an autoimmune response.
5. Remove the toxins from our environment, our food and our bodies.
6. Eat the right foods to nourish your body.
7. Take the necessary supplements to support your health.
8. Address any underlying infections.

We can achieve the above outcomes by making the necessary changes in various aspects of our lives. I created the *Nine Pillars of Hashimoto's Health* to help you take informed action:

1. **Support**: the team of people you put together to help and support you on your road to wellness.

2. **Mindset**: having the right mindset as you start your journey to health.
3. **Medication**: replace the thyroid hormones with the right medication for you, support your immune system with natural remedies and address underlying infections.
4. **Meals**: eat the right food to heal your gut and help you feel better, eliminate the food that triggers an immune response or leaky gut.
5. **Sleep**: improve your quality of sleep as a key part of managing your stress as well as giving your body rest and opportunity to recover.
6. **Stress**: stress management to reduce the rollercoaster ride of cortisol and adrenaline in the body when exposed to stressors all the time.
7. **Toxins**: remove toxins from your body and your environment.
8. **Movement**: enjoy the exercise that you do.
9. **Supplements**: the supplements needed to support your healing and energy levels.

In the next chapters, I will give you information supported by scientific research and a toolkit of action steps. You can decide where you want to start based on what you believe you struggle with the most. Then move on to the next pillar. You don't have to do all the actions I have listed here in the order that I have documented them. You can change the order of actions to best suit your life and circumstances.

These are also not the only actions you can take. As research on autoimmunity is completed and published, and we see advancements in technology and medical breakthroughs, what we can do to improve our health may change or there may be additional actions we can take. Please don't see this book and the actions here as the "everything-you-need-know book", as what we know may change. This is my guideline based on many years of experience in the hope that you will benefit from my 'trial and error' along the way.

Always remember this: *Do your research.* You are your own best advocate – don't let any doctor tell you it is all in your head. There is no one right way – do what works for you. If you fall off the wagon, be kind to yourself and catch that wagon. Be kind to yourself always. Take each day, day by day. This is the start of your journey to attain better health. I have achieved this and you can too.

CHAPTER 6: PILLAR 1 - SUPPORT TEAM

Being diagnosed with Hashi's is a very personal experience, and it can also be a very lonely one as you are trying to get to grips with what is happening in your body. My husband Johann, as supportive as he was, could not fully comprehend the impact and the debilitating symptoms. I often felt so guilty that there were more times than I care to remember that I couldn't participate in our family – simple things like making dinner. Later, it was frustrating (to me) to see that the things we used to love to do, like spending time outdoors and taking the dogs for a walk, were simply too much for me. And sadly, we stopped doing them.

Your journey to health should not be a lonely path. One of my favorite quotes is by Marie Forleo, and it is "*everything is figureoutable*". I love this quote, because it means that you are not a victim, you can figure everything out, if you want to. And herein lies the first lesson…

You must become the CEO of you and your health

Your health is yours to own and to be in-charge of. You need to take charge of your life and your health. No one else can do it for you. You need to find the best team to work with you and support you. Find the right people to be on your team and fire those who are not right. You must take the power of your health in your own hands and own it.

Your family-and-friends support team

Living with an autoimmune disease is not easy, and every day you are on a journey towards better health. Your close family is your first support line, and it is important that they understand what is happening with you, and how they can help you. Educate them, teach them, guide them - and forgive them (when you have to). Don't keep them out of the loop. When you are not feeling at your best, you need them.

There have been many days where I just didn't have the energy to do anything, and my husband Johann simply took over to ensure that dinner was made for the family and the house was (sort of) clean. Of course, I too had to learn that "what he does is good enough" – and let go of perfection!

My circle of friends also understands and supports my journey. They know that I cannot have gluten, and they are not offended if I bring my own prepared food to their homes (if needed). It is not an issue, and because they are my friends and have my well-being at heart, they do not make it an issue.

Some family and friends may think you are overreacting and disregard your dietary requirements or support needs. While the natural reaction may be to get angry, I want to advise you to let it go. It just isn't worth trying to convince them otherwise.

In 2019 after I left my job, my body crashed, and I slept for almost three months. It was insane. I had no energy, absolutely none. My husband and daughter were the ones who truly supported me during this time. Without their support, it would have been really challenging. And then…

The other important element of family and friends is to surround yourself with **positive and supportive** friends and family. I cannot emphasize this enough – negativity is destructive and not needed in your healing journey! A negative family member or friend can inflict a lot of frustration and stress in your life. When you are focused on making changes, there is no space for negativity.

In fact, what you need are cheerleaders! I love the term cheerleader as a support mechanism! Imagine a group of cheerleaders – they are supporting you, cheering you on, saying things that motivate you and tell you that you can do it! That is what you need in your family and friends. And then….

A community of Hashi's warriors

One of the best places that I have found my cheerleaders, are in online groups. You can find a group of cheerleaders in many of the social media platforms. Look for a group that is positive and supportive, that shares information and tips and ideas.

I have often shared my frustration, my feeling-like-a-failure, my desperation and even my sadness online with fellow Hashi's warriors. They have supported me in times when I felt so lonely in my journey, because only others who have Hashi's can truly understand what you are going through and can empathize with you.

If you cannot find a group you like, create your own group online where you can build a community of support for yourself and for others.

And then…

You too can be a cheerleader for someone else. We all go through the emotions of "I can do this!" to the other side of "I can't anymore". You can provide support for someone else who might be feeling down and overwhelmed. I have found that many times I know something that can help someone else – a tip, a suggestion – which not only helps them, but makes you feel better too!

Remember that you are not alone. You don't have to be alone. Connect with others, get support and give support.

Your medical support team

Your medical team is a crucial part of your support structure. Getting to the right doctor who listens to you, respects your journey and who wants to partner with you to help you get to the root issues, can be a long and frustrating road. I have "fired" many doctors, including specialist physicians and endocrinologists, as they were only treating the symptoms and not helping me to find and fix the problem. So here is my recommended list of medical practioners:

A functional doctor is very different to an allopathic (conventional) doctor. Allopathic or conventional doctors are trained to look at the symptoms and to diagnose and prescribe accordingly. The focus is on disease diagnosis and treatment of the symptoms. They are not trained to look at what the root causes could be that led to the symptoms in the first place. With Hashi's, they will usually prescribe the synthetic medication or more aggressive treatment options like radioactive iodine or even thyroid surgery to remove the thyroid (which is often the treatment options for Grave's disease, the hyperactive thyroid autoimmune disease). Please take note: conventional doctors are very important when you have acute attacks in that they can intervene when, for example, you experience a thyroid storm and intervention is needed to save your life. But they have not been trained to help you find the root cause that led to your immune system going awry and attacking your thyroid gland in the first place.

A functional doctor has a different view and looks at your body holistically – what is going on, not just in terms of the physical symptoms that you may be feeling, but also what is going on in your life that could contribute to the body's burden, as well as what are you using as fuel (the food you eat).

The challenge you will face is two-fold: finding a functional doctor, and secondly, finding one that you resonate with and can work with. I am a big believer that you must like the people who you bring into your life, and that their energy must complement your own. Think about this for a moment. It's not about going to see the "best" doctor

– you must find the **best doctor for you**. Someone who will listen to you, someone who will keep asking questions, and someone who cares about how you are feeling. This is the ideal doctor you want to bring into your team.

A **biological dentist** is the next person I recommend you have in your team. A biological dentist is a dentist who also considers the impact of what happens to the teeth and mouth on the rest of the body. They work with materials that are compatible to the body, as each person is different in which materials they can tolerate and how well they can tolerate them. If you have amalgam (silver) fillings or other dental work done, a biological dentist will take the necessary precautions to ensure that no vapors or material in your mouth trigger an autoimmune response.

A **health coach** is also a great addition to your support team, specifically for support in between the visits to your functional doctor. A health coach can also advise you on the lifestyle changes you should make and they will provide you with both mental and emotional support.

A **nutritionist and/or dietician** who understands autoimmunity can also be of great support, especially if you need help with specific health issues, like healing your gut or dealing with nutrient deficiencies. Most people see a dietician only when they are looking to lose weight, and it is here where the experience with Paleo, AIP and other programs are valuable. A nutritionist or dietician should also be able to work out a plan for you based on your health and your lifestyle.

And then there are **other health modalities**. As our bodies are complex and our lives are busy and demanding, do not underestimate the support you can get from other health modalities, including physiotherapy, homeopathy, chiropractor, acupuncture and other modalities. Depending on where you are in your healing journey and the challenges you face every day, you may benefit from incorporating other modalities in your support network. Always be honest about what you are eating and avoiding, the medications you are taking (prescribed, over the counter, herbal and homeopathic remedies), as well as supplements.

Furthermore, never feel guilty if you see someone else that your doctor does not support or agree with. It is your body and your journey, and just because someone else doesn't believe in a modality, doesn't mean it cannot and will not work for you! You do what you truly believe is right for you.

Action Steps

1. **Find your medical support team.**

   I recommend you find a medical doctor who has been trained in functional medicine to help you. Functional doctors are trained to find the cause of the symptoms. They will spend more time with you to understand your symptoms, reduce the impact of your symptoms and ultimately put Hashi's in remission. Other medical doctors include a biological dentist, as well as dietician or nutritionist should you need it.

2. **Find an autoimmune health coach for guidance and support.**

   A health coach can be a great support during your healing journey. A health coach can help you with implementing lifestyle changes, give support and keep you accountable.

3. **Inform your family and friends about Hashi's and discuss your boundaries.**

   Inform your family and friends of your autoimmune condition, including what they can do to support you. Share with them that although you may look fine, it is not always how you feel. Be factual without being apologetic or trying to justify your choices. If your family and friends understand, then great! If not, don't try to convince them or need them to understand, because, unless they have a chronic illness, they might not understand. Also explain to them the changes you are making (for example, avoiding gluten and dairy), so that they can support and help you.

They may not fully understand how you feel and the impact that Hashi's has on your life, but they do need to respect the boundaries that you are putting in place to protect your health and your energy.

4. **Find and online group for support.**

   If you cannot find one, start one yourself. Being part of a community is an important step on your healing journey. You can find support groups online for autoimmune diseases or groups specifically for Hashimoto's Thyroiditis. Become part of the group and participate, asking questions, asking for help when you need it and giving support to others. The biggest reason I believe in support groups is the understanding that we are not alone.

CHAPTER 7: PILLAR 2 – MINDSET

There are two ways you can view your Hashi's condition: it is a gift, or it is a curse. How you view it will have a huge impact on your path to health.

There is an important link between your mind and your body. Author and stem cell biologist, Bruce Lipton, describes it this way: '*Your brain controls the biology in your body*'.

Let's take the example of falling in love – which is all about the emotion of love and happiness. The brain gives the instruction to the body to release the most amazing happy hormones – dopamine, oxytocin and growth hormones, and you literally glow from the inside!

Take the other side of this spectrum: the emotion of fear. Our bodies were designed a million years ago to react to fear with a fight-or-flight response. Your brain immediately goes into action – releasing the protection hormones of cortisol, adrenaline (nor-epinephrine) and inflammatory agents called cytokines, to get you to fight or run. It does this by contracting the blood vessels in your core (where all your important organs are), and literally forcing the blood away from your core into your arms and legs, so that you can fight or run! Your digestion and immune systems shut down in the effort to divert energy and blood to the arms and legs.

Not so great when you already have immune system challenges!

My concept of how your mindset influences your journey towards healing Hashi's has a few components to it:

1. How are you viewing this 'thing' that has happened to you? Is it a positive or negative experience?
2. What is your health goal? What do you really want? In order to answer this question, you need to really reflect on what is important to you as it will influence you.
3. How are you spending your time? Your need to rest and recharge will be higher when you have a flare up, and so you will need to make some decisions about what is important to you and what you are spending your precious time and energy on.

You can decide how you want to view this *thing* that you have: you can see it in a positive light, or you can see it as a negative disease. Think about it for a moment: when your brain detects an emotion of fear and distress, it puts your body in distress mode. If you see it as something you can work with and see it as an opportunity to make changes in your life, your brain, and therefore your body, will respond appropriately.

Can you view your Hashi's diagnosis as a positive thing that has happened to you?

A positive choice

I think you can. Here is why:

1. **It's a wake-up call for your health**. This can be just what you need to get your stuff in order. How did you come to this point? Did you constantly eat crap food, survived on as little sleep as possible, worked hard and played just as hard? No exercise? Come on, be honest here. You don't just wake up one day with an autoimmune disease. Also, you can't come to me with the excuse that it is in your genes. Remember epigenetics? Only about 1% of disease in the world is caused by genetics. The rest is all lifestyle and beliefs. Hashi's is your red-light warning to get your health and life in order.
2. **It's telling you to evaluate your life**. Enough of this being busy all the time and pushing for more. Hashi's really is a great opportunity to ask these questions: what are you doing? What are you chasing? What is chasing you? Why are you doing what you are doing? Is this really what you want to do? Why are you so stressed? Why have you chosen to be so stressed? Perhaps it is time to make a different choice.
3. **It's telling you to rest, recover and recharge.** This is one I am guilty of. I feel guilt when I sit and do nothing. There is always stuff to be done, work that needs attention, others to look after. When you run out of fuel, running on fumes is not good for you. Your body will tell you very loudly and clearly if you have worked too hard, over-exercised, or even played too hard! It will force you

to rest. So why not be proactive about it, and say no to things that sap your energy, and say yes to sleep, reflection and pause.

4. **It's telling you to fuel your body with nutritious, healthy food.** There is no such thing as junk food – it is either junk or it is food. Choose wisely. With Hashi's your gut is not working the way it should be, food is not digested, nutrients are not absorbed and inflammatory elements are leaking into the body. When you eat only nutrient-dense healthy food, you give your body the right fuel, the right nutrients and you heal your gut!

You have a choice to make. You have Hashi's, that is done. How you view it is entirely up to you and it will make the biggest impact on how you move forward from here. If you choose to see it as a punishment, you will find the food choices limiting, you will not listen to your body and force it to do more than what it can. It will be hard, and it will be a struggle.

View this as an opportunity to get your health back. Some things may work, and other things may not! It is not to say that this will be easy – but do you really want to choose the alternative - a journey of suffering? Some days will be hard, you will feel tired, overwhelmed and demotivated. But don't get stuck there. You can feel better. You can reclaim your life. Here is how I believe you can achieve this: be informed, make small changes regularly. And herein lies the next point…

Adopt a "get-better" mindset

What is your mindset? Do you feel hopeless and overwhelmed, or do you feel you can make changes and learn?

Heidi Grant Halvorsen, author of the book *The 8 Motivational Challenges*, describes two mindsets: Be-Good and Get-Better. When you have a Be-Good mindset, you are reluctant to ask for assistance as you should have the ability to do it. But what is more important, is that when you have a setback, you react in one of two ways:

1. You freak out, are anxious as you "don't have what it takes", or
2. You just give up, deciding that you don't have what it takes, and with feelings of hopelessness and being overwhelmed, you stop putting in the effort.

With a Get-Better mindset, you have the belief that you can develop your ability, you can learn new skills and you can make progress over time. The key focus here is progress.

Why is this so important? With a Get-Better mindset, you will not be rattled when you experience a difficulty. You realize that you will make mistakes along the way and that you will learn from them, making you better, stronger, grittier. I am not sure if there is such a word, but just go with it!

With Hashi's, you must own a Get-Better mindset. The alternative is not an option. Being diagnosed with Hashi's and learning to make the changes necessary so that you can live a healthy, fulfilling life, is hard. Adopting a Get-Better mindset is what will help you – you can learn how to reduce the impact of a flare-up, you can seek help for guidance and support, and you can make the changes so you can have energy, health and vitality. It's about progress.

As you start to feel better, a little every day, it will give you the motivation to keep going. With support groups, you can follow the steps of others who have taken this journey, and soon, you will support others who are taking their journey to health.

Action Steps

1. **See Hashi's as an opportunity.**

   Decide to see Hashimoto's Thyroiditis as something that you can work with and see it as an opportunity to make changes in your life to be healthier.

2. **Adopt a Get-Better mindset.**

   This is a journey, and you will need to find what works for you and what doesn't. It's about progress, not about being perfect. This is a journey to figure out what works for you, and you will experience a few bumps and detours along the way. Just keep going forward and catch that wagon when you fall off.

CHAPTER 8: PILLAR 3 - MEDICATION

In this chapter we'll look at the different medications and natural remedies than can support your immune system and your thyroid, namely:

1. Thyroid hormone medication
2. Low Dose Naltrexone
3. Herbal remedies
4. Addressing underlying infections

Let's quickly talk about the idea of medication. There seems to be an approach by many doctors and the pharmaceutical industry that there is a "pill for every ill". There is more awareness about the misuse of medication than in the past, and patients are more mindful of the impact of medications on their health and are looking for other options to heal before considering taking pharmaceutical drugs. And rightly so. I too have taken an approach to seek alternative remedies before taking pharmaceutical drugs.

Today, I am taking thyroid hormones and I make use of natural remedies to support my immune system. I want to give the information to you so that you can make an informed choice which may just make all the difference in your life!

Thyroid hormone replacement

The word "medication" is not really the right word to use when looking at the thyroid medications doctors prescribe. The reason is that many people have a view that they don't want to take medication. I had a conversation with a recently diagnosed Hashi's patient, and she was adamant that she did not want thyroid medication and wanted to heal her thyroid naturally. While the goal seems aspirational, I believe it is the wrong way to think about it. For many of us, being diagnosed with Hashimoto's Thyroiditis comes after a long period of not feeling well and after consulting with many doctors. During this time, it may be that your thyroid has been damaged to the extent that it simply cannot produce the number of thyroid hormones that your body needs. It is therefore necessary to help your thyroid and supplement it with the right number of thyroid hormones so that you can live the life you want – with energy, vitality and health.

Medication is valuable and useful if it works, if it does more good than harm, and if there are no other non-drug alternatives that can achieve the same results. And this is exactly where thyroid hormone supplementation comes into the story: it can save your life. If your thyroid hormones are too low, you are not healthy. You cannot be healthy. Period.

Thyroid blood test panel

Your doctor will likely request a range of blood tests to determine which level of thyroid hormones you require. The thyroid blood test panel your doctor should request include the following:

- TSH
- Total T4
- Free T4
- Free T3
- Reverse T3
- TPO antibodies
- Tg antibodies

Let's have a look at each of these blood tests.

TSH (thyroid stimulating hormone) is the hormone that the pituitary gland releases to instruct the thyroid gland to produce thyroid hormones. A high TSH level may indicate that the thyroid is not producing enough thyroid hormone (underactive thyroid). It is as if your body is asking for more and the pituitary gland is giving the instruction, but the thyroid gland just cannot make enough. A low TSH level may indicate that the thyroid is producing too many thyroid hormones (over-active thyroid). In some cases, a low TSH may be because of an abnormality in the pituitary gland, which prevents it from making enough TSH to stimulate the thyroid. A low TSH may also occur if you are taking T3 hormones, which can suppress the TSH. There are also two types of TSH tests: normal TSH and sensitive TSH. Always ask for the sensitive TSH, which will require you to fast for 12 hours before the test.

Total T4 measures the total amount of the T4 hormone in your blood. When the T4 is low, it may be due to insufficient T4 production by the thyroid, or that the TSH levels are not high enough to instruct the thyroid to produce more thyroid hormones, meaning there could be a problem with the pituitary gland.

Free T4 is a test you must do every time you check the effectiveness of your thyroid treatment plan. This test measures the level of T4 that is not bound to a protein in the blood and is one of the most important tests to determine how well the thyroid is working. This is the amount of T4 that is available for conversion to T3 by the liver, the gut and the cells. People with hyperthyroidism (over-active) will have elevated FT4, while people with hypothyroidism (under-active) will have low levels of FT4 when they are first diagnosed with an underactive thyroid or with Hashimoto's Thyroiditis.

It is when you combine the TSH test with the FT4 test that you start to understand what is happening with your thyroid:

- When you have a high TSH and low FT4, it indicates hypothyroidism due to low production levels of the thyroid hormone by the thyroid. The higher TSH indicates that the body is requesting more thyroid hormones, the pituitary gland is giving the instruction, but the thyroid simply isn't making enough for the body's needs.

- When you have a low TSH and a low FT4, it indicates hypothyroidism due to a problem involving the pituitary gland (not releasing enough TSH for the thyroid to act on).
- When you have low TSH and a too high FT4, it indicates hyperthyroidism (over-active thyroid). The thyroid gland is producing T4 hormones without guidance from the pituitary gland, which is also a problem and could even indicate Grave's disease.

Total T3 measures the total amount of T3 in your bloodstream. When the levels are low, it may indicate poor thyroid function, or a problem with the conversion from T4 to T3.

Free T3 measures the T3 hormones that are not bound to a protein in the bloodstream. It is the view from this test that is helpful in diagnosing hyperthyroidism (overactive thyroid).

Reverse T3 (rT3) is an inactive form of T3 that the body cannot use. It takes up space and blocks the active (free) T3. Levels can become high during times of major trauma, surgery or severe chronic illness. This test is usually much more expensive compared to the other tests and there is controversy around the value of this test. The test is not generally recommended for routine evaluation of thyroid health. There are some who believe that there is value in this test, particularly when a patient is taking thyroid medication and not feeling better. It is about the ratio of Free T3 to rT3: a low ratio can indicate a problem that the body is trying to conserve energy to fix a problem (but it cannot tell you what the problem is). There has not been a lot of research about rT3 outside of an intensive care unit, so discuss this with your functional doctor when you want to do this test.

If you are experiencing extreme stress, I would suggest adding Reverse T3 to the blood tests, as it can indicate what is causing your low levels of T3. Your body may be converting the T4 hormones into the useless Reverse T3 hormones.

TPO Antibodies is an antibody test that measures thyroid peroxidase antibodies, and it may indicate the presence of an autoimmune disease (Hashi's or Graves). However, if the results are low or absent, it doesn't mean that you don't have an autoimmune disease - it just means that is not present at the time of the test. This test can confirm an autoimmune disease, but it can't exclude it. Sometimes a person may have an autoimmune disease and it won't be picked up by the blood test.

Tg Antibodies is an antibody test that measures the thyroglobulin antibodies. A negative test only means that there are no antibodies at present. It doesn't rule out an autoimmune disease.

Once you have your blood test results, you should review them with your doctor and then discuss and decide on the best options. In the next section, we'll review the options available for replacing the thyroid hormones your thyroid cannot produce anymore.

Thyroid hormone replacement options

As your thyroid become less and less functional with each autoimmune attack (where healthy thyroid cells are damaged and become ineffective in making thyroid hormones), it is important to replace the missing thyroid hormones. There are two thyroid hormones that are typically prescribed:

- T4 replacement, called levothyroxine. In South Africa the two brands are called Euthyrox™ and Eltroxin™. In the USA it is marketed under brand names such as Synthroid™, Levoxyl™, Tirosint™, while in Canada it is Eltroxin™. In Australia the names are Oroxine™ or Eutroxsig™, while in Europe you will find Euthyrox™.
- T3 replacement that can be used alone or in combination with levothyroxine.

T4 or levothyroxine is a man-made (synthetic) hormone. It is the most prescribed thyroid hormone medication. The belief is that the body will convert the T4 into the T3 as needed. The challenge is when you may be taking the right amount of T4 medication, but the body is not converting it to the usable T3 hormone. Therefore, it is important to always test for Free T3 as well when checking the levels of the thyroid hormones in the blood, as you may still feel symptomatic even with Free T4 levels within normal range.

T3 is another synthetic hormone that can be used as a stand-alone hormone therapy, or in combination with levothyroxine. There are two sources of T3 available:

- Synthetic T3, which is liothyronine. In the USA it is marketed under Cytomel™, Triostat™, Levoxyl™, and Levothroid™. In South Africa it is marketed as Tertroxin™. This hormone is also used to treat goiter (enlarged thyroid) or as a support treatment to thyroid cancer therapy.

- Natural desiccated thyroid, shortened as NDT, which is a combination of T4 and T3, and it is derived from the dried glands of pigs or cows. Currently desiccated thyroid extract is made from pig thyroids and is available as Armour Thyroid™, Nature-Throid™ and WP Thyroid™ in the USA. In South Africa, compounding pharmacies can provide NDT. Some people believe it is a more "natural" treatment. I have a concern about the quality regulation of this drug, as it is not controlled or regulated.

Most experts agree that many people with hypothyroidism do very well with T4 alone. However, there are clearly some people who benefit from combined approach. If symptoms continue while you are on T4-only medication, it may be worthwhile discussing a combination treatment of T4 and T3 hormones or only T3 hormones.

I used to be on the T4 hormone and a T4/T3 combination hormone (product called Diotroxin™). This product was discontinued in 2016, and I immediately felt the impact. I felt more lethargic and emotional, and I slowly started to gain weight. The endocrinologist who I went to see in desperation for help, continued me on T4 thyroid hormones only, even though I asked for T3 hormones. It was only in 2019 that my functional doctor immediately started me on T3 hormones that I started to feel like myself again!

One piece of advice: never stop or change your thyroid hormone replacement (medication) without talking to your doctor about it. Thyroid hormones are 'called' the Goldilocks hormones – you need the right amount and the right combination for you. It may be very tempting to take more than what you need, especially since weight-loss is one of the side effects of an over-active thyroid. But this can be very dangerous, as it can lead to what is called a "thyroid storm", where there is too much thyroid hormone in the body. It can have devastating effects, including brain damage and slipping into a coma.

One of the challenges in many of the thyroid medication brands, is the inclusion of fillers to make the tablet. It is highly frustrating for Hashi's patients when fillers like corn (in Armour™) are used, or lactose (in most thyroid medication except Tirosint™, WP Thyroid™ and combination medications). Do you see the irony here of avoiding dairy and then there is lactose in the medication? If you are concerned about a possible reaction to a filler, always speak to your doctor about it and see if there are any possible alternatives.

If you are experiencing the symptoms of a Hashi's flare-up, speak to your doctor as soon as possible. Also, be very careful with dosage changes. You may be in a temporary state of hyperthyroidism (too many thyroid hormones in your body). Remember that you are dealing with hormones. Don't make any huge adjustments in your dosage, as it can be a shock to your body and make you feel much worse. When you and your doctor are tweaking the dosage, make sure you follow up with the blood lab analysis every three months.

This can be very frustrating, but remember you are taking a potent hormone, so slow is the way to go.

Remember that big pharmaceutical companies also promote their patented medications over the unpatented/off-patent T3 medications, as there is more money in it if for them if patients buy the patented medications.

Normal blood panel results vs. Optimal blood panel results

When you receive your blood test results from the lab, the report will indicate the normal ranges for each test. If your results are within the normal lab ranges, your doctor may tell you that your results are normal and there is nothing more to do. This is the time when I want to ask you to please not just accept it, as there is a huge difference between what "normal" lab ranges are and what the optimal ranges are for people who have Hashi's. While an allopathic doctor may tell you that your results are within the normal ranges and nothing more can be done, a functional doctor will take a very different approach, and will be looking at optimal ranges for people with Hashi's.

What is normal for the general population may not be optimal for you. Your results may still be in the "normal" ranges as the lab defined it, but you may still be feeling the symptoms and not be feeling well at all. You don't need to be "normal"; you should be "optimal". These two concepts are not the same thing. A functional doctor will work with optimal ranges.

Another important point is that "normal" ranges may differ from lab to lab, depending on the equipment and process each lab uses to analyze the blood. So if you use different labs (different companies), you may find that you struggle to know if you are actually improving or worsening. If possible, ty to use the same lab for your blood tests over a period of time, so that you can track and compare your results and see what is happening with your autoimmune markers and your thyroid function.

How do you know if you are at your optimal level of thyroid hormone medication? Well, it is as simple as asking: how are you feeling? If you are feeling great, you have energy, you can think clearly, and you can work on your dreams and goals, I think that is a very good indicator that you are at your optimal level of thyroid hormone supplementation.

But what if you are not feeling great? It may be that your thyroid hormone supplementation is too high or too low, which brings its own symptoms for each side. Dr Isabella Wentz created a list of symptoms that you may experience if you are either over-treated or under-treated with thyroid hormone supplementation:

Symptoms if under-treated	Symptoms if over-treated
o Apathy o Brain fog o Cold intolerance o Eyebrow thinning / loss	o Agitation o Excess sweating o Heat intolerance o Insomnia o Irritability

Symptoms if under-treated	Symptoms if over-treated
o Fatigue	o Mood swings
o Hair loss	o Palpitations
o Heavy periods	o Rapid heart rate
o Joint pain	o Restlessness
o Puffy face	o Scant periods
o Sadness	o Weight loss
o Tangled hair	
o Weight gain	

If you are not feeling well and suspect that you may be over- or under-treated, tick the symptoms above that apply to you and consult your doctor. Remember, if you do adjust the thyroid hormone dosage, keep it to a small change and repeat the blood tests in three months to see how they are changing.

Keep track of your blood test results

As you start your journey towards the life you deserve, it is important to track your blood test results so you can see the impact of the actions you are taking. You will see how the values change over time and will be able to address any deficiencies or changes. It also makes it easy for a doctor to review your history of blood results.

Use a spreadsheet on your computer to track your results. I suggest you include the following information: the date of the blood test, the level of thyroid hormone supplementation you are on, any supplements you are taking regularly, your stress level, TSH level, Free T4 level, Free T3 level, TPO level, TgAB level, Reverse T3 level (if being tested), any other results (like vitamin D, ferritin, cholesterol, insulin, etc.), and which lab did the test. I also recommend you include space to note your doctor's comments, and your own observations about actions you have taken.

When to take your thyroid hormone pills for optimal absorption

Most people should take their thyroid medication first thing in the morning on an empty stomach. I too have been advised to take my thyroid hormones first thing in the morning on an empty stomach and to wait at least 30 minutes before I drink or eat anything. Interestingly, some people have reported that they feel better when taking their thyroid medication in the middle of the night. You need to find out what works best for you, as there is no one-size-fits-all approach. And always take your thyroid hormones as your doctor prescribed it.

Why should we take the thyroid hormones on an empty stomach? One simple reason: to make sure that as much of the thyroid hormones are absorbed as possible. The absorption of the thyroid medication can be impacted by several things:

- **Stomach acid level.** If you have low levels of stomach acid (a condition called hypochlorhydria) or no stomach acid (a condition called achlorhydria), you may have impaired absorption of the thyroid hormones. If you experience bloating, burping, heartburn, diarrhea, indigestion, hair loss, fatigue, nails breaking and gastrointestinal infections, you may have low levels of stomach acid. Please consult your doctor about diagnosis and treatment options. Treatment options may include HCI supplements (like betaine with pepsin, berberine or digestive enzymes) or antibiotics (if the underlying cause is an infection). In some cases, digestive bitters (a natural stomach stimulant) may help.

- **Medications and supplements.** Antacids, calcium, magnesium, aluminum, iron and PPI's (proton pump inhibitors) can all lead to suppressed stomach acid. Therefore, you should take these supplements and medications at least four hours after you have taken your thyroid hormones. Also keep in mind that if you are taking calcium and iron supplements, that you take them at different times of the day since calcium and iron block each other if you take them together. It is recommended that you take iron in the afternoon and calcium with dinner. If you are taking magnesium, I recommend you take it at bedtime. Also, the absorption of the synthetic T3 hormones, like Cytomel™, can be impacted by oestrogen-based contraception, antacids as well as cholesterol-lowering drugs. Other pain and anti-inflammatory medications such as NSAIDS (nonsteroidal anti-inflammatory drugs like aspirin and ibuprofen) can also lower thyroid hormone concentration in the body, principally by interfering with the binding of T4 and T3 hormones to the proteins in the blood. Rather use paracetamol for pain and fever.
- **Food**. Most people can take their thyroid hormones first thing in the morning, on an empty stomach, wait 30 minutes, and can

then have breakfast. If you find that your dosage needs to be increased (and you didn't have a flare up) or your lab results are not consistent (even though you have been on a consistent dosage), it may be that you need a longer period between taking the thyroid hormones and eating food. You may have to wait an hour, or even take your thyroid medication during the night or a split dosage during the day. Before you make any changes, consult with your doctor.

- **Coffee**. Coffee interferes with the absorption of thyroid hormones. Wait at least 30 to 60 minutes to drink your coffee, if you are having that morning expresso! Remember that ideally, you want to avoid dairy, so if you really cannot go without your daily caffeine, keep it to black coffee!
- **Gut problems**. Gut problems like celiac disease, lactose intolerance, infections, parasites or even atrophic gastritis (a chronic inflammation of the stomach lining), can reduce the absorption of thyroid hormones. Consult your doctor about treatment options to reduce the impact so you have maximum absorption of your thyroid hormones.

Thyroid hormone medications and thyroid panel blood tests

The general rule of thumb for blood tests are these: don't eat or drink anything for 12 hours before the blood tests, make sure the test it is done between 8 and 9 o'clock in the morning, and finally, only take your thyroid hormone replacement medication after your blood has been taken.

The reason for this is about the duration of the impact on the body, also known as the "half-life" of the medication. It describes how long it takes for half of the dose to be metabolized and eliminated from the bloodstream. Then there is also the time it takes from when you take the medication that it is at its highest point, and this is the reason why we wait and only take the thyroid medication after the blood has been drawn.

Low Dose Naltrexone

Low dose naltrexone (LDN) is a medication that has been beneficial for many to help modulate the immune system without the severe side effects that other similar medications may have. It was originally used in the 1980s to help patients with opioid withdrawal and to help treat alcoholism. Doctors then found that when this drug was used at extremely low doses, it seemed to help with modulating the immune system, and therefore improving the health of patients who have autoimmune diseases. Great news, right? Maybe.

How LDN works

Opioids are products like morphine, heroine, tramadol and hydrocodol (Vicodin™). The theory is that naltrexone goes and blocks the places where those drugs work in the human body. When it is used in small dosages compared to the traditional dosage, the naltrexone partially blocks the receptors in the brain, and it has an interesting effect: the body increases endorphin production. It also increases the receptors and the sensitivity of the receptors, and it has an immune modulatory effect. The naltrexone does not suppress the immune system, but it helps it to work correctly – so that neither the Th1 nor Th2 immune helper cells are taking over. The term used by doctors is that the low dose naltrexone helps to "modulate" the immune system.

Doctors recommend that you take LDN at night before you go to sleep. It blocks opioid receptors in your cells during the first 2 to 3 hours of sleep. So, when those receptors are shut off during sleep, it signals the body to give an influx of endorphins.

Should you consider using LDN?

While research on LDN is limited (as the drug is off-label and no pharmaceutical company would be able to patent the medication), the anecdotal evidence for using LDN is strong. Some people with Hashi's experience tremendous benefits, such as less pain, more energy and lower levels of antibodies. Some people have even been able to eliminate all their Hashi's symptoms, and depending on which stage they are in, may even stop taking thyroid hormones.

LDN works for some, and it doesn't work for others. Consult with your doctor about introducing LDN for you, especially if you have multiple immune conditions, have a high level of thyroid antibodies or experience many symptoms. LDN is only available on prescription.

Dosage and reactions

The dosage of LDN for use in autoimmunity situations is recommended to be 2 to 4,5 milligrams, starting at 2 milligrams and building up the dosage over a period of a few weeks. The reason you want to do this is to avoid what happened to me: a reaction. I started with the full dosage of 4,5 milligrams on my doctor's advice, and about a month in, I started getting ill and despite being on antibiotics, I got another illness a week later and another a week later. I went to see my family doctor three times in three weeks, which was very unusual! The only thing that changed in my life was the LDN, and so we stopped the LDN. We believe that starting on the full dosage of LDN didn't work for me, and it likely caused a herx reaction.

The herx reaction is short for the Jarisch-Herxheimer reaction. What happens is that with a treatment (say antibiotics or LDN in my case), there is a release of bacterial toxins into the bloodstream as the microorganisms die because of the treatment. This dumping of toxins then causes a reaction. In my case, I became sick with infection after infection and my immune system couldn't cope with the demand that was placed on it. Taking further antibiotics to deal with the infection probably didn't help! So, I definitely recommend starting with a lower dose and increasing it over time.

Another reported side effect is vivid dreams, which could disrupt your sleep if they wake you up, but the dreaming should subside after about two weeks.

When you take LDN, make sure you do regular blood tests: First, there might be an impact on the liver, so when you are taking LDN, please do regular liver function tests. This medication is also not a life-long medication, meaning that once the immune system is in balance again, you should be able to stop using LDN.

LDN can also cause hyperthyroidism. The reason is that as the immune system calms down, the thyroid may now start to create thyroid hormones, and if additional thyroid hormone supplementation is taken, it can be too much for the body and you can become hyper. If you do experience hyperthyroid symptoms, immediately contact your doctor.

Herbal remedies

Herbal remedies may not be part of the allopathic treatment plan, since the allopathic approach is limited to prescribing levothyroxine, NDT or a synthetic T3 hormone. When you want to include herbal therapy in your healing journey, it is important to remember that any herbal supplements you use cannot replace the thyroid hormones that your damaged thyroid is unable to produce anymore. I want to stress this again: herbal supplements cannot replace the thyroid hormones and it cannot rebuild the thyroid gland tissue that has been damaged. However, when used correctly, herbal supplements can help to calm inflammation and help with managing and decreasing symptoms.

Reduce inflammation and modulate the immune system

The herbs which are great to help with inflammation and for modulating the immune system are *calendula* (Calendula officinalis), *ginger* and *cinnamon*. These herbs are great in helping the immune system down-regulate inflammation. Two herbs that help with supporting the Th1 and Th2 immune system cells are fresh *chicory* and fresh *dandelion*. These herbal leaves can be easily added to salads and other savory dishes.

Supporting the thyroid and reducing thyroid antibodies

Your body needs to be able to convert the inactive T4 hormone to the active T3 hormone that the body can use. It is also important to focus on reducing the thyroid antibodies.

One of the herbs that has gained attention is *black cumin seed*. At the time of writing this book, I have not yet tested it, so I'll share the research that has been done on this herb. There have been two studies done recently about the impact and effectiveness of black cumin seed on people who have Hashi's. The first study found the following results:

- Improved body mass index, as well as reduced waist and hip circumference,
- Improved thyroid function by a decreased TSH, and
- An increase in T3 hormone and a decrease in the TPO antibodies (thyroid peroxidase antibodies).

The other exciting study was done on 40 people with Hashi's who had elevated TPO antibodies. This study found the following results:

- Lower LDL and triglycerides (bad cholesterol) and an increase in HDL (good cholesterol),
- A decrease in TSH and TPO antibodies, as well as a slight increase in available T3 hormone.

There are a few ways in which you can take black cumin seed. It doesn't taste good, so look at your options and which one will work best for you, then buy the form that works best for you. First, you can grind up your own seeds every day and consume the equivalent of 2 grams a day, but this process can be a lot of effort and may not be practical. Second, you can buy a highly concentrated cold-pressed organic black cumin seed oil. This can be in soft-gel form, or in a glass jar. Third, you can make a tea by pouring hot water over 1 tablespoon of black cumin seeds and steep it for 10 minutes. Fourth, if you drink a protein shake, you can add 1 tablespoon of the seeds to your shake.

When looking at buying a black cumin seed supplement, make sure you purchase an organic, quality product by a reputable producer. The soft-gel option is probably best due to the bad taste of the oil. Avoid purchasing oil that is a glass jar, as you don't know how much light exposure it had, which can lead to oxidation of the oil.

A word of warning: a 2010 study showed that black cumin oil inhibits two key enzymes used to metabolize about 75% of pharmaceutical drugs. So, if you are taking any other prescription drugs, please check with your doctor before you start taking it.

Supporting the liver

The liver plays a key part in converting about 60% of the inactive T4 hormones to the active T3 hormones. There are herbal supplements to support the liver. Bitter herbs help to support the liver, and you can take them as drops, making it very easy to take throughout the day. Bitter herbs include *gentian, burdock root, chamomile, dandelion root* and *goldenseal.*

Helping with decreasing the body's stress response

Some herbs act like adaptogens (an adaptogen, as defined by the Merriam-Webster dictionary, is 'a plant extract that is known to help increase the body's ability to resist the damaging effects of stress and promote or restore normal physiological functioning'). These herbs can help foster stress resilience and bring a sense of calm and balance throughout the body. Some examples are: *ashwagandha* (Indian ginseng), *rhodiola* (golden root), *chamomile, licorice, astragalus* and *tulsi.* These herbs are great at lowering cortisol levels. But if your cortisol levels are low, you could be making yourself feel much worse if you take cortisol-lowering herbs.

Just note that ashwagandha is a member of the nightshade family, and if you are considering an elimination diet or have sensitivities to nightshades, this herb may not be the right one for you to use.

Increase glutathione

Schisandra berry is a great herb to increase glutathione. Glutathione is an antioxidant, and in dealing with any autoimmune disease, you want to increase your glutathione levels. One way to increase your glutathione intake is to eat more protein. Another way is to take a selenium supplement. It also acts as an anti-viral, antihistamine and helps to protect the liver.

Herbs you should avoid

Herbs to avoid in general: *lemon balm, motherwort* and *cannabis.* These herbs inhibit the conversation of T4 to T3.

Address underlying infections

Infections can hide just about anywhere in the body, including your thyroid gland. One of the problems we have is that pathogens may have a similar structure to the cells of the thyroid gland, while others can infect the thyroid gland.

If you suspect you may have an underlying infection that could be causing your symptoms, consult with your doctor to do the necessary tests The tests may include blood tests, stool antigen or breath tests. Some of the more common infections are:

- Epstein Barr virus (which causes mono) has been strongly correlated with multiple sclerosis (MS), chronic fatigue syndrome (CFS), lupus and Grave's Disease.
- E.coli
- Herpes Simplex 1 and 2 (gives you cold sores and/or genital herpes)
- Lyme disease caused by a bacteria
- Human parvovirus
- Blastocystis hominis
- Mumps
- Rubella
- Sinus infections

- SIBO (small intestinal bacterial overgrowth)
- Hepatitis C

If you do have an underlying infection, work with your doctor to treat it.

Action Steps

1. **Optimized thyroid hormone medication.**

   I recommend you work with a functional medical doctor (licensed doctor who is trained in functional medicine) to optimize your thyroid hormones. Thyroid hormones need to be optimized specifically for you, and the normal lab ranges are not applicable. I strongly recommend that you seek out a functional doctor to work with, as he/she will work with you to make sure you are on the thyroid hormones option that is best suited for you, whether it is synthetic T4, synthetic T3 or desiccated T3 hormones. Never change your thyroid hormone dosage without first speaking to your doctor about it. Please be aware that this is not a quick process and will take some time to understand what the optimal dosage is for your body.

2. **Request a full thyroid panel when you go for blood tests.**

   The tests I recommend you do are TSH, Total T4, Free T4, Free T3, TPO antibodies and Tg antibodies. You may also want to include Reverse T3 if you have been under severe stress.

3. **Track your blood test results.**

   If you have done thyroid blood tests in the past, request the results from your doctor or the lab. Use spreadsheet software on your computer to create a template and start to track the values of the different tests. As you do blood tests, add the latest results to the tracker. You can also include space for your doctor's comments and recommendations, as well as your own observations.

4. **Use paracetamol for pain and fever.**

   Check your medication and remove NSAIDS (nonsteroidal anti-inflammatory drugs) like aspirin and ibuprofen. Use paracetamol for headaches and other pains. NSAIDS for pain and inflammation relief can lower thyroid hormone concentration in the body, principally by interfering with the binding of T4 and T3 hormones to the proteins in the blood.

5. **Limit or avoid using antacids and antihistamines.**

   Antacids and antihistamines can affect the gut microbiome and can lead to leaky gut. Speak with your functional doctor about other treatment options if you have acid reflux, hay fever or other conditions that require these medications.

6. **Consider incorporating herbal therapy to support your healing journey.**

   Herbal therapy can assist your body to reduce the impact of stress, calm inflammation and support the immune system. Remember to research the herbal remedies as some may react to your medications and other conditions you may have. Please consult with an herbalist to help. Always inform your doctor about any herbal therapy you are using.

7. **Consider low dose naltrexone therapy.**

   Low dose naltrexone (LDN) is a medication that has shown beneficial results in helping to modulate the immune system. It is an off-label drug, and you will need to have a prescription to get it. It has varied results, working very well for some people, and not at all for others.

8. **Address underlying infections.**

   An underlying infection may trigger a flare-up. If you suspect you may have an underlying infection – anything from a sinus infection to a viral or bacterial infection, I recommend you consult with your doctor to seek diagnosis and treatment.

CHAPTER 9: PILLAR 4 - MEALS

Food is personal. Food is social. And while we have to eat every day, I have found that changing habits around food is often the most difficult to achieve. It should be the easiest thing to change as we have to eat every day, but we have beliefs and deeply-ingrained habits about food. We have food that we like and dislike, and religious beliefs also play a role for many people. The food we eat has a huge impact on our health.

Also, we are bombarded with information about diets, latest research findings and advertisements about the "healthiest" food, and it is a challenge to distinguish what is fact and what is fiction! And then there are claims about superfoods and supplements that help us to curb our appetites and is the next weight-loss silver bullet. No wonder it is overwhelming and confusing! Low-fat, low-carb, slow-carb, keto, vegan, Pegan, Paleo, vegetarian, raw-food, FODMAP, GAPS, Mediterranean, alkaline, AIP, low calories, anti-inflammatory, and the Elimination diet to name a few. Some based on science, some total science fiction.

What do you do if you have Hashimoto's Thyroiditis and you want to eat food to support your health?

In this section we'll be going back to basics about nutrition and have a look at what the scientific research says, as well as the experiences of other Hashi's patients. Of course, there will be foods that are highly recommended that you avoid, and we'll discuss those as well. There are many books dedicated to the topic of food that support healthy thyroid function. The idea is not to replicate those authors, but to give you an idea of the options that you have, and what has worked for others.

The point is this: there is no one perfect diet. There is no one perfect way to eat. Everyone is different, and what works for one person may not work for you. Finding out what works for you may take time and will be trial and error. A nutritionist and/or dietitian who understands autoimmunity and Hashimoto's Thyroiditis can be of great help. Nutritionists understand food on a molecular level and can create meal plans that are able to identify dietary elements that trigger symptoms.

In this chapter, we will look at the foods that cause inflammation. Often, by eliminating these foods you can reduce the inflammation. I'll also share what has worked for others. What you won't find here is a recommended diet and recipes.

Let's start with the foods that are known to be inflammatory. If you want to calm inflammation, start here.

Foods that cause inflammation

We want to avoid the foods that cause inflammation in the body that burden our immune systems. Here is the list of foods that cause inflammation in the body. If you want to reduce the inflammation in your body, these are the foods that you should avoid:

1. Gluten,
2. Other grains,
3. Dairy,
4. Soy and soy products,
5. Legumes,
6. Sugar,
7. Alcohol,
8. Coffee,
9. Nightshade vegetables, and
10. Food high in iodine.

It may feel that there is nothing left for you to eat and enjoy, but I assure you, there are a wide variety of foods available to you! Let's first go into the detail of why I recommend that you avoid the foods listed above, and why it should be on your avoid-list as well.

1. GLUTEN

You may have read that gluten is the first thing that you should cut from your diet. But what is gluten, and why should we avoid it? Gluten is a word that labels a range of proteins found in the seeds of grains. One of these proteins is called gliadin, and this protein is causing the problem.

There are three issues with gluten. First, gliadin has an effect on intestinal permeability (leaky gut) and can activate the immune system. Second, gluten contains phytic acid, which binds to minerals in your body and stops your body from absorbing these minerals, specifically iron, zinc and calcium. So, you can experience nutrient deficiencies. Third, gluten contains lectin. Lectin acts as a natural pesticide for crops and can wreak havoc on the lining of your gut. Many believe that gluten is the primary trigger of leaky gut because it releases the chemical zonulin in your intestines, telling your gut lining to "open". Lectin can then enter the bloodstream, and the immune system kicks into action to get rid of it, leading to inflammation.

But there is more bad news: there's also a convincing case that lectin contributes to leptin resistance, which makes you gain weight. Leptin (not to be confused by lectin which is a natural pesticide for plants) is a hormone that helps to regulate satiety. Leptin is released by the fat cells in your body, telling the brain that the body has enough energy in storage and you should stop eating. But if the brain is not "reading" leptin, it is called leptin resistance, which is a "brain-is-starving-but-the-body-is-obese" situation.

Where do we find gluten? Gluten is in wheat, wheat germ, rye, barley, bulgur, couscous, farina, graham flour, semolina, spelt, triticale, and kamut matzo. Just think about everything you eat, like bread, cakes and pastries. Sadly, gluten is found in just about all processed foods!

The first step recommended for autoimmune patients is to avoid gluten. Which means you have to **never** eat gluten again. This is hard, but not impossible. It will take a little creativity from your side, and a little research about alternatives. For example, almond nut flour is great for bakes, while arrowroot powder is a perfect substitute for maize flour to thicken sauces. Many restaurants offer gluten-free pizza and pasta, so you can still enjoy meals out with family and friends. A word of warning: be careful of gluten-free alternatives that are available, like gluten-free muffins and breads. These products are often loaded with sugar, which is not great if you want to lose the extra weight. Some gluten-free foods may also have other hidden inflammatory ingredients, like soy and soy derivatives, even casein and whey (derivatives from milk). Just because it's gluten-free, doesn't mean that you can eat it!

Keep in mind that manufacturers love to use terms to create more sales. Think about this: water is gluten free, fruit is gluten free, vegetables are gluten free, meat (like steak) is gluten free. So, there is a lot of food that you can label gluten-free! It doesn't make any sense at all!

Can you enjoy gluten occasionally? Unfortunately not. You cannot be 90% gluten free. You are either gluten free or you are not. Every time you eat gluten, you risk triggering your immune system. Did you know that it can take up to six months for your body to remove the gluten? It is just not worth it to eat foods that contain gluten.

There are so many products that have wheat and gluten as an ingredient, so you really must look at the ingredients carefully. It can be very challenging to remove gluten - even toothpaste has gluten in it! Most of the synthetic T4 medications have wheat or gluten in as part of the filler ingredients. Gluten can be disguised on labels under different names, as well as included in other products: the more familiar names are brown rice syrup, caramel color (often made from barley), dextrin, hydrolyzed malt extract, hydrolyzed soy protein, hydrolyzed vegetable protein, maltodextrin, modified food starch, natural flavoring, yeast extract. Other names are Avena sativa cyclodextrin, fermented grain extract, hordeum distichon, hordeum vulgare, hydrolysate, phytosphingosine extract, samino peptide complex, secale cereale, triticum aestivum, triticum vulgare, tocopherol / vitamin E.

2. OTHER GRAINS

There are other grains that you should also avoid, like rice, quinoa, buckwheat, oats and corn. Even though these grains do not contain gluten, these grains can be cross-reactive. These grains contain a high content of inflammatory lectins (which is a natural pesticide for plants) and phytic acid. Phytic acid binds important minerals along with them, and over time can deplete your mineral stores, specifically iron, zinc and calcium.

Rice is gluten-free and many people believe it is a great replacement as a starchy carbohydrate. The problem with rice is that it absorbs a huge array of heavy metals when it is grown, including cadmium and arsenic. These are heavy metals that interfere with magnesium and calcium to work appropriately. Another reason to avoid rice is because of how rice is processed. After the rice is harvested, it is processed with an industrial enzyme to prolong the shelf life. This enzyme is called mTg, that stands for Microbial Transglutaminase. Research has shown that this enzyme is immunogenic (meaning it creates an immune response) in people who have Celiac Disease, also an auto-immune disease.

Gluten-free oats are an alternative to oats. Gluten-free oats are usually grown in separate dedicated fields, so cross contamination with normal oats and wheat fields should be limited. But gluten-free oats do have a similar protein to gluten called avenin that can damage your intestinal lining if you're sensitive to it. Oats are also susceptible to mold, so the recommendation by post-Hashi's patients is to avoid it.

Corn contains a gluten-like protein called zein that can damage your gut lining. Corn is also one of the most genetically modified foods around and is heavily sprayed with pesticides. It is often also high in mold and mycotoxins. If you have a leaky gut and inflammation, I recommend you avoid corn.

3. SOY

Soy is a staple used in many pre-prepared meals. It is cheap to grow and process, and therefore is used as a filler in many products, even cosmetics! Soy produce includes soy lecithin, soy sauce, tofu, tempeh, and edamame beans (which is the young soybean). Vegans and some vegetarians often turn to soy and soy products as an alternative source of protein.

The problem with soy is that it is a highly inflammatory food and it is also a goitrogen. This is a new word that we haven't discussed yet. Goitrogens are substances that suppress the function of the thyroid gland by interfering with thyroid hormone production. When you read up about goitrogenic foods, you may find that some people recommend you avoid all goitrogenic foods, and others will say that there are goitrogenic foods that you can eat (like broccoli). Soy however is one goitrogenic food that you need to cut out completely and immediately.

What about organic soy? Is this a healthy option? Most of the soy grown is GMO - genetically modified. Whether the soy is organic or GMO, it doesn't matter. It still has the same impact on the thyroid: it suppresses and interferes with the thyroid's function.

Soy can be disguised under a variety of names. Here are names you should look out for: bean curd, soy lecithin, shoyo, miso, tamari, gum arabic, carob (unless it is not made with soy lecithin), hydrolyzed vegetable protein, hydrolyzed soy protein, tofu, tempeh and of course, anything with the word "soy" in.

4. DAIRY

Milk, cheese and cream - many of us have grown up with dairy as a staple in our diets. We have been told that dairy contains vital nutrients like calcium to maintain healthy bones. But is this really true?

There are a variety of foods that will provide your body all the calcium it needs, like kale, oranges, collard greens, broccoli, figs and spinach. Along with incorporating these foods into your diet, you can always add in a calcium supplement. We'll talk about supplements in a later section.

Dairy causes inflammation in many people, either due to lactose intolerance (the sugar in milk) or casein and whey sensitivities (protein in milk). Another problem is that dairy is typically also full of hormones and antibiotics (that was given to the cows to prevent and treat disease). Some of the potential symptoms that could indicate a dairy sensitivity are gas, bloating, acid reflux, irritable bowel syndrome, asthma, sinus congestion, skin breakouts or ear infections.

It is time to cut the dairy.

5. LEGUMES

Legumes are pulses and beans. The better-known legumes include alfalfa, clover, peas, chickpeas, lentils, lima beans, soybeans, carob, peanuts, tamarind and other beans. While legumes are often a staple and are generally considered healthy, if you have an autoimmune disease, you should avoid them. Let's look at why.

Legumes contain lectins, which act as a natural pesticide for crops and can wreak havoc on the lining of your gut. Chris Kesser, a health coach, stated that most of the lectins in legumes are destroyed when they are cooked. So while the problem might not be with the lectins, the problem with legumes are with the carbohydrates. Legumes are part of a group of foods that is referred to as FODMAP. Another new term we need to understand. FODMAP stands for "fermentable oligo-, di-, mono-saccharides and polyols". It is a type of carbohydrate that is resistant to digestion and is not absorbed into the bloodstream. When this type of carbohydrate reaches the end of your intestines, where your gut bacteria use the carbs for fuel, it produces hydrogen gas and can cause digestive symptoms in sensitive individuals. Another side effect of FODMAPs is that they draw liquid into the intestine, which may cause diarrhea. Not pleasant at all.

Chris Kesser also mentioned that legumes are not very nutrient dense. Here's how I interpret this: when you want to give your body fuel and the ability to heal, you want to give your body food that is full of nutrients. Legumes therefore, are not that food. So perhaps not the best food choice for when you are on the journey to get your health back.

6. SUGAR

Sugar is evil. Really. Sugar not only makes you fat, it also makes you sick. The consumption of sugar has been linked to diabetes, heart disease and liver disease. The biggest problem with sugar is that it is hidden in so many manufactured foods.

Let's quickly have a recap on sugar, and which ones should be avoided. In biochemical terms, sugars are the building blocks of carbohydrates. The more specific terms are glucose, fructose (the sugar found in fruits) and lactose (the sugar found in dairy). Sucrose is also problematic, and it includes the man-made sugar high fructose corn syrup, which is super sweet and used in food manufacturing. It's all these added sugars which is causing huge problems with your health.

The problem with sugar is that it is everywhere. Many people eat very high amounts, both deliberately and unknowingly. Many people deliberately add sugar to their coffee or cereal, and if you drink many cups of coffee a day, it all adds up! Then there are the hidden sugars in foods such as bread, yoghurt and carbonated drinks. When you start reading labels, you will notice how sugar is added to just about everything that is made in a factory!

Many people think that low-fat and fat-free foods are healthy, but the truth is that after the processing to get it to be low-fat and fat-free, it doesn't taste like much and sugar is added to make it tastier. A significant amount of sugar is added!

But how bad is sugar really? A study published in JAMA Internal Medicine showed that your risk of dying from heart disease increases with the proportion of sugar you have in your diet. This study was conducted over 15 years. Participants who ate 25% of their calories in added sugar were twice as likely to die of heart disease than those who ate less than 10% added sugar.

Sugar is also very addictive. With the huge amount of sugar that is included in our foods, many people eat too much sugar without realizing it. Sugar has the following impact on your body:

1. **It causes your glucose levels to spike, then then to plummet**. Because of this spike and fall in your blood sugar levels, you can

have mood swings, fatigue and headaches. The more sugar you have, the higher the risk of obesity, diabetes and heart disease.

2. **It can affect your immune system**, as it interferes with the way that your body fights disease. Bacteria and yeast love sugar, and by eating sugar, these organisms can build up and cause infections.
3. **Sugar causes tooth decay by helping the growth of bacteria and plaque**. It can also cause gum disease.
4. **Sugar can wreak havoc on your body** and can make it very difficult to progress on your journey of Hashi's health. If you can steadily decrease your reliance on sugar, or even cut it out immediately, you will start to feel better.

First, read, read, and then read some more. Read the labels of everything you buy. Even the pre-mixed spices have sugar listed! Sugar can be disguised under different names on labels, making it very hard to understand how much sugar has really been added.

Second, cut the sugar from your coffee and tea. Also, cut the dairy as well if you haven't done so already. Dairy has a ton of hidden sugars that add up with each cappuccino you drink!

Third, check your definition of "healthy" foods. Many foods that are considered healthy, are loaded with sugar. Yoghurts, breakfast bars, breakfast cereals and store-bought fruit juices are typically "healthy" foods which are packed with added sugars. These are not healthy at all.

What if you have that craving for something sweet? What works for me when I have a craving for something sweet is reaching for a fruit, like a banana or fresh dates, a small piece of dark chocolate (with a cacao content of 80% or higher), or a freshly made cacao smoothie!

Whoa, stop the boat! Fruit? Doesn't fruit contain high amounts of sugar? The sugar in fruit, which is a natural sugar, is not the same as the processed sugar. The body also doesn't digest fructose in the same way as it digests processed sugar. When you eat a fruit, it contains fructose, soluble and insoluble fiber as well as minerals and vitamins. The fiber helps to slow down the absorption of fructose in the digestive tract. Fruit, and in particular, fruit juice, has been given a bad rap – often being blamed as spiking glucose levels. Yet, studies have shown that fruit juice is a great way to obtain essential nutrients and phytonutrients, and even 100% fruit juice does not have a significant impact on blood glucose levels or insulin levels and therefore fruit juice is not associated with an increased risk of diabetes.

But for the rest of sugar? Just cut it out.

61 DIFFERENT NAMES FOR SUGAR

Want to know the 61 different names for sugar? Here they are: agave nectar, barbados sugar, barley malt, barley malt syrup, beet sugar, brown sugar, buttered syrup, cane juice, cane juice crystals, cane sugar, caramel, carob syrup, castor sugar, coconut palm sugar, coconut sugar, confectioner's sugar, corn sweetener, corn syrup, corn syrup solids, date sugar, dehydrated cane juice, demerara sugar, dextrin, dextrose, evaporated cane juice, free-flowing brown sugars, fructose, fruit juice, fruit juice concentrate, glucose, glucose solids, golden sugar, golden syrup, grape sugar, high-fructose-corn syrup, honey, icing sugar, invert sugar, malt syrup, maltodextrin, maltol, maltose, mannose, maple syrup, molasses, muscovado, palm sugar, panocha, powdered sugar, raw sugar, refiner's sugar, rice syrup, saccharose, sorghum syrup, sucrose, sugar (granulated), sweet sorghum, syrup, treacle, turbinado sugar and yellow sugar.

7. ALCOHOL

The rules are not so clear cut with alcohol as with many of the other foods. Some believe you should completely avoid it, while others believe that some alcohol, like red wine, is good for you because of the antioxidants it provides.

Researchers have found that frequent alcohol consumption increases the amount of gut toxins in the bloodstream, and high levels of these are linked to chronic inflammation and can even lead to organ failure. Then there are studies that claim that a moderate amount of alcohol can protect against autoimmune diseases, like Hashi's, while another study by Cambridge University claims that it is difficult to identify the impact of alcohol on the body as there are too many factors to consider.

Some diets will completely limit the use of alcohol, while others will allow white wine, and others red wine. If you want to have a drink, keep the following in mind:

- Limit your in-take of wine as the sugar can be high.

- Check the ingredients. Some alcoholic beverages are grain-based (like beer) which can sap your energy. It may also have added dyes and artificial flavorings.
- If you must have wine, keep to low-alcohol, low-sugar wine if you can.

8. COFFEE

If you are like me who loves a cup of coffee in the morning, this may be one of the hardest things to hear: coffee really isn't good for you if you have Hashi's. There are a couple of reasons.

First, coffee is one of the foods that is heavily treated with herbicides to protect the crops. Second, coffee beans can be a source of mold in the way that coffee beans are stored. Third, coffee can deplete the body of minerals, like magnesium and zinc, and these two minerals are important for a healthy functioning thyroid.

Coffee, unfortunately, will be on the avoidance list when you are recovering. There are great alternatives to coffee that you can explore, such as teas and chicory.

9. NIGHTSHADE VEGETABLES

Nightshade vegetables are a group of vegetables that belong to the Solanaceae family. It includes regular white potatoes, eggplant, tomatoes, goji berries and peppers (both bell peppers and the eye-watering chilies). It also includes the spices that are made from these plants, including paprika, red pepper flakes and cayenne pepper. There is a more toxic plant as well, the belladonna plant, which can kill a human. Black pepper is not in this category as it comes from a different plant.

Let's have a look at why nightshade plants may be problematic for some people. First, nightshades have a natural pesticide, a group of chemical compounds called alkaloids. One of these alkaloids is solanine, and another is capsaicin (which gives peppers the heat!). These alkaloids act as a "bug spray" while the nightshade is alive, defending it from pests and molds that would otherwise kill it. In other words, these nightshades are designed to be toxic. The alkaloids are also more concentrated in the stems and leaves of the nightshades, which are the parts we don't eat. People with a healthy gut can handle these chemicals without a problem, but people with a compromised digestive system or an autoimmune condition like Hashi's, may experience problems. When eating these alkaloids, it can increase the body's immune response, which is exactly what you don't want. The chemicals may also irritate the gut lining, leading to leaky gut (intestinal permeability) and then an immune reaction.

Second, nightshades also contain lectin, which can also be a gut irritant in many people. Lectin is a type of protein. Nightshades contain large amounts of lectins which could elicit the same response as alkaloids in people who are sensitive to nightshades. Lectins are also considered to be anti-nutrients, since they can negatively affect the body's ability to absorb nutrients. Lectins also contribute to intestinal permeability (leaky gut), which adds to inflammation in the body as other bacteria move from the gut into the bloodstream.

The good news is that cooking destroys many of the lectins. That is why tomatoes can be great to use once cooked.

Even if you don't show any sensitivities to nightshades (like skin rashes, itching, excessive mucus production, achy muscles and joints, ongoing and unexplained fatigue, bloating, gas, heartburn and migraines), it is recommended that if you have an autoimmune disease, that a 30-day nightshade elimination is definitely something you should consider. Slowly then re-introduce these veggies to check if you show any sensitivity symptoms. Also, people who experience gut problems may need to consider avoiding nightshades.

10.FOODS RICH IN IODINE

Iodine is controversial and should be considered carefully before you supplement with it. Iodine is a necessary element that the thyroid needs to make thyroid hormones. It may seem logical that if you are hypothyroid you should supplement with a high dose of iodine, as then the thyroid will have enough to make thyroid hormones. But is it the right way to think about iodine supplements?

Many people with hypothyroidism are given the advice to supplement with iodine as the belief is that the underactive thyroid is caused by an iodine deficiency. But taking additional iodine can be a very bad idea. Dr Edwin Lee (Board Certified Endocrinologist practicing Functional Medicine) explained that iodine is a controversial supplement. If you have positive thyroid peroxidase (TPO) antibodies (thus Hashi's with TPO antibodies), and you take high doses of iodine, you risk destroying your thyroid faster. What happens is that thyroid peroxidase attaches iodine to make thyroid hormone, and if you have a positive thyroid antibody and you put more iodine in, the positive antibodies will use the iodine and decrease the function of thyroid peroxidase.

Research has also shown that excess iodine is a risk factor in the development of Hashi's, and in some cases, a low-iodine diet can be helpful in reducing the attack on the thyroid and normalize thyroid function in people who have iodine-causing Hashi's.

So more is not always better.

Can you eat goitrogens and cruciferous vegetables?

Foods that contain goitrogens have been given a very bad rap. Cruciferous vegetables, like bok choy, broccoli, brussels sprouts, cabbage and cauliflower, have been put on the avoid list because it is believed that these foods contain glucosinolates, which may block iodine absorption into the thyroid gland. But this is only a problem if you have low iodine levels, and most people with Hashi's do not have an iodine deficiency. So, you can enjoy these vegetables. Cruciferous vegetables are only truly goitrogenic in a raw state AND if you eat a huge amount of them, so if you are concerned about your iodine levels, just make sure you lightly steam or ferment these vegetables.

Mind your macro's and micro's

When we look at food and diets, we need to understand about macro and micronutrients. Macro means "large", and it is these nutrients that we need in larger quantities for growth, repair, energy and health. There are three macro nutrients: protein, fat and carbohydrates. There is a fourth bonus one: water. We need these four macronutrients every day.

Micronutrients is the term used to describe vitamins and minerals in general. Vitamins and minerals play a very important role in energy production, immune function, growth, bone health and many other processes.

Proteins

Proteins provide your body with the essential amino acids it needs to keep healthy. Amino acids are the building blocks of cell and muscle structure. There are 20 types of amino acids, and nine of them are essential (meaning that your body cannot make them, you need to take them in from your food). Your thyroid gland uses certain amino acids to create the thyroid hormones and that protein also helps support a healthy immune system.

The best sources of protein are meat, fish, poultry, eggs, dairy and soy-based products. Beans, nuts and lentils also contain protein, but it is incomplete, meaning that each have some of the essential amino acids, but not all of them. With Hashi's, we need to avoid dairy and soy. We need to focus on high-quality, organic (antibiotic free) meat, fish, poultry and eggs. With some of the diets that are recommended for people who have Hashi's, eggs are recommended to be avoided, like with the Auto-Immune Paleo approach.

Fats

Fats are important for brain development, making hormones and helping with the absorption of certain vitamins (A, D, E and K). Fats also help keep us feeling fuller for longer (increased feelings of satiety). However, not all fats are created equal.

There are different types of fats:

- **Saturated fats** are present in foods such as hard cheese, cream, butter and visible fat in red meat. Coconut oil, palm oil and cacao butter are also saturated fats. These are also termed "solid fats", as the fat is solid at room temperature. There are also a lot of saturated fats in processed foods, particularly trans fats, and partially hydrogenated oils, that are in many fast foods and manufactured baked goods. These are very bad for your health. Trans fats are chemically processed fats to enhance the shelf life of the fats and make food taste better, yet it is very unhealthy. We must avoid anything that has trans fats and partially hydrogenated oils.
- **Unsaturated fats** are found in plants, oils, nuts, seeds and fish. These types of fats are usually liquid at room temperature. Unsaturated fats can further be categorized into monounsaturated fat and polyunsaturated fats. Monounsaturated fat is found in avocado and seed oils such as canola, olive and peanut oil. Polyunsaturated fat is found in mainly found in vegetable oils such as safflower, sunflower, sesame, soybean and corn oils, as well as seafood.

The more important distinction with polyunsaturated fats is the difference between omega-3 and omega-6 essential fatty acids. You'll see again the word "essential", which means that the body cannot make these fats and you must take them in as part of your food. There is also omega-9 fatty acid, which is a monounsaturated fat and it is not "essential", meaning that this fatty acid can be produced by the body.

I want to focus on the omega-3 and omega-6 essential fatty acids. Omega-3 essential fatty acids are very beneficial to your health: they improve heart health, support mental health, decrease fat in the liver, support infant brain development and most importantly, they help to fight inflammation.

Omega-6 essential fatty acids are primarily used for energy, but these types of fats are also pro-inflammatory. It is an essential fatty acid, so the body does need it, but not in the quantities that most people consume it!

What we need to look at is the amount of omega-3 and omega-6 fatty acids that we consume. With processed foods, the amount of omega-6 fatty acids far outnumbers the amount of omega-3 fatty acids, and herein lies the problem. With the high amount of omega-6 that we eat, from foods like mayonnaise, soybean oil and corn oil, we contribute to the inflammatory reaction in the body.

We need to focus on reducing the intake of pro-inflammatory omega-6 fatty acids and increase the intake of anti-inflammatory omega-3 fatty acids. The best foods for increasing your intake of omega-3 fatty acids are oily fish (such as salmon, mackerel, sardines and anchovies), chia seeds, walnuts and flaxseeds. The fats to avoid, which add to your omega-6 fatty acids intake are vegetable oils such as canola, sunflower, soybean peanut and corn oil.

But this also opens the conversation about which oils we should be using in our cooking. Coconut oil, extra-virgin olive oil, avocado oil, walnut oil and macadamia nut oil are all great options for cooking with. Let's have a quick overview of each of these oils:

- **Coconut oil** has a very high smoke point, making it very stable at higher temperatures, and thus the ideal oil to use for frying. Even though coconut oil has a very high level of saturated fats, there are studies that suggest that coconut oil can increase the HDL in your blood (the "good" cholesterol) without increasing LDL (the "bad" cholesterol).
- **Extra-virgin olive oil** is very high in monounsaturated fats and low in polyunsaturated fats. Olive oil is not ideal for frying, as it has a relatively low smoke point. It also becomes very unstable at high temperatures. Olive oil contains powerful antioxidants, helps fight inflammation and protects your blood cholesterol from oxidation.
- **Avocado oil** is just as heart healthy as the actual avocado. It is rich in omega-3 fatty acids, monounsaturated fat and oleic acid. This is a very versatile oil. You can use it cold in salads and dressings, heat it for cooking as it remains stable, and even use it for skin treatments and to help heal injuries. It contains lutein (which is

good for your eyes), antioxidants and vitamins that reduce dry, itchy and flaky skin.

- **Walnut oil** is expensive and has a limited shelf life of six months to one year. It is great to use on salads, as flavoring for steaks and fish, and can even be used in desserts. Walnut oil is full of antioxidants, it helps improve blood flow to your hair follicles and can help to prevent hair loss.
- **Macadamia nut oil** is perfect for cooking as it is stable as high temperatures. It has a much longer lifespan than walnut oil and can be kept for up to two years in the refrigerator. It has one of the highest levels of monounsaturated fats compared to the other oils, and it has a 1:1 ratio of omega-3 to omega-6 fatty acids.

Carbohydrates

Everything else, which is not a protein or a fat, is a carbohydrate. Grains, vegetables and fruits are all carbohydrates. Carbohydrates consist of starch and sugars which the body breaks down into glucose, the main source of energy for the body. Your body can also store glucose in the form of glycogen in the liver and muscles.

But not all carbohydrates are created equal.

Vegetables can be divided between starchy and non-starchy vegetables. Starchy vegetables include potatoes, sweet potatoes, butternut, beetroot and peas, while non-starchy vegetables include all the dark-green leafy vegetables (like spinach and kale), broccoli, cabbage, cucumber and celery to name a few.

Fruits generally are higher in carbohydrates than vegetables, but even with fruit there are fruits with a lower carbohydrate content, like berries (strawberries, blueberries and raspberries) and fruits with a higher carbohydrate content like pineapple, apple, dates, raisins and banana.

Grains are all higher in carbohydrates than vegetables and fruits. This will include all forms of baked breads, oats, pasta, cereals and beer.

And let's not forget sugar. There are many different forms of sugar, and we have already discussed sugar. Even the healthy natural sugar, like honey, agave nectar, maple syrup and coconut sugar, are all still carbohydrates.

Water

Water does not contain any calories or nutrients, but it is considered a macro nutrient as we need water for our bodies to function. Water is critical for our health, as it helps to bring nutrients to the cells and removes waste from the body. Water also helps to regulate your body temperature and helps with metabolism.

How much water do you need to take in? The Institute of Medicine recommends that men should drink about three liters of water, while woman should drink about 2.2 liters of water. Keep in mind that your water intake can vary according to your activity level, medical conditions and your level of consumption of coffee and alcohol (which are dehydrating).

So why do we need to know about macro nutrients? For one simple reason: so that we can be aware of what we eat. It's that simple. I believe we should eat as naturally as possible. These are foods that you can identify in their natural and unprocessed states and that do not come in packaging with a barcode. This includes meat, chicken, fish, fresh vegetables, fresh fruits, raw nuts and seeds, and healthy oils like olive oil and avocado oil. Remember, there is no such thing as junk food – it's either junk or it's food.

Is there a diet that is best for Hashi's?

I am often asked if there is a diet that is best for when you have Hashimoto's Thyroiditis. I wish I could tell you to simply just follow one diet and all will be well, but unfortunately it isn't that simple. Our bodies are complex and we deal with different challenges, and then there are personal likes and dislikes, as well as religious beliefs and beliefs about food. Again, what works for some, may not work for you.

In researching what diet works best for when you have an autoimmune disease, there seem to be certain recommendations. Many people feel better by going gluten-free. The Paleo approach is also highly recommended, as it avoids most of the common inflammatory foods. In the online support group, some ladies have reported that they finally feel great and have lost weight by following a diary-free low-carb-high-fat diet, while others have reported that the ketogenic diet has worked for them. Others have recommended doing low-carb-high-fat combined with fasting. Some ladies have recommended that after changing to Paleo and you still don't feel better, the AIP (autoimmune Paleo) or the Elimination Diet could help to find your food triggers.

The point I am trying to make here, is that there isn't a perfect diet.

When looking at a diet, which I define as 'a way of lifelong eating', you are going to have to figure out what works for you in terms of your body, your beliefs and your ability to keep going with it. I have developed my own principles for healthy eating and I will share them with you:

1. **Eat real food.** Eat whole food. A steak, a fruit, a vegetable. It's that simple. Avoid processed foods and anything that comes in a packet with a label and ingredients that you need a scientific degree to understand.

2. **Avoid the inflammatory foods.** Gluten, soy and dairy are the common culprits that can cause havoc with Hashi's patients. Also, avoid legumes, coffee and alcohol. Cut the refined sugar.
3. **Enjoy vegetables and fruits.** Juice it, eat it raw, cook it, roast it! Aim for 10 portions, which is approximately 800 grams, of fresh fruit and vegetables each day.
4. **Cut the crap.** Junk food and fast food is not food. There is junk, and there is food. Eat food.
5. **Incorporate healthy fats.** Enjoy olive, coconut and avocado oil. You can also enjoy avocado, chia seeds, walnuts and flaxseeds.
6. **Enjoy ginger, turmeric and garlic.** These foods are well-known for their anti-inflammatory properties.

7. **Make it work for you.** Dr. Roger Williams came up with the term Biochemical Individuality. It is that we are all individuals with different requirements that will help us be healthier. Keep in mind that we also have our personal beliefs, other medical conditions, tastes and preferences as well.

Below is a short overview of each of the most popular dietary approaches, and there are many resources available online that can help you with recipes. I also recommend that you find a dietician or nutritionist that is familiar with autoimmunity to help you. In the meantime, here is a short summary of the most popular dietary approaches:

The Gluten-Free Diet is often the first step in dietary changes for autoimmunity. Avoid anything that contains gluten, which includes wheat, rye, barley, couscous and even oats. Be cautious of baked goods labelled "gluten free", as they are often loaded with sugar and other carbohydrates like rice, soy and potato flour. You may not be eating gluten, but the high carbohydrate content may contribute to your weight-gain problems.

The Paleo Diet is focused on only eating foods that our Paleo ancestors ate. It removes the foods that man introduced in the last 10 000 years. A Paleo-style diet is a great place to start with eliminating foods that generally cause digestive issues, and focusing on real, whole and nutrient-dense food sources. Paleo diets tend to be higher in healthy fats with moderate amounts of protein and generally fewer carbohydrates, but Paleo is not necessarily a low-carb diet. One of the dangers of going Paleo is reducing your carbohydrates too much, because the most common sources of carbs are generally forbidden, and if you are struggling with thyroid or adrenal problems, eating the Paleo way can put additional stress on the body.

The Autoimmune Paleo Diet (AIP) is based on the Paleo principles and focuses on excluding those foods which cause inflammation. It is designed to help heal a leaky gut and dysbiosis that have resulted in systemic inflammation and an autoimmune condition. It was developed by Dr. Loren Cordain and Robb Wolf, then modified further by Dr. Sarah Ballantyne. AIP is great for anyone who has gut issues and/or an autoimmune condition and for those who continue to struggle after eating Paleo for some time. The idea is to eat AIP for a period of time, and then start to reintroduce foods and see if any foods are triggers for autoimmunity to flare up. Those foods that causes a reaction are then avoided from there on.

The Low-Carb-High-Fat Diet (LCHF) aims to limit the consumption of starchy and sugary foods and unhealthy fats, and get the body to burn fat as a source of energy instead of the carbs that you eat. This is a high fat, moderate protein and low carbohydrate way of eating. This diet has proven to work well for people who have metabolic diseases like diabetes. The LCHF diets have gained huge attention in recent years, particularly with the research done by Professor Tim Noakes. Low carb diets can be very effective for certain medical conditions, including overweight and obesity, type 1 and 2 diabetes, epilepsy, PCOS, high blood sugar, metabolic syndrome, Parkinson's and Alzheimer's disease. There is, however, preliminary research coming out now that ketogenic and very-low-carb diets may cause adverse changes to gut bacteria.

The Food Sensitivity or Elimination Diet is focused on figuring out which foods you react to, and then eliminating those foods from your diet. You can do a blood test for food sensitivities or eliminate these foods for a period of 30 to 90 days then slowly reintroducing them to see what you react too. The biggest challenge with this diet is to have patience and dedication, as it can take time to slowly reintroduce foods and see which ones you react to. Typical foods that are excluded are gluten, dairy, soy, sugar, artificial sweeteners, corn, peanuts, eggs and shellfish, tomatoes, all citrus and fruit juices, sugar, chocolate, coffee, black tea, alcohol, soy and yeast. Also, this diet should only be done for a period of time and then you should start to reintroduce foods.

The **Low FODMAPS Diet** was developed by researchers at The Monash University in Australia. It's just a fancy name to describe a class of sugars and carbohydrates that are found in certain foods (Fermentable Oligo-Di-Monosaccharides and Polyols), and to focus on eliminating these from your diet. Some people have experienced that these sugars and carbs can cause a range of gastrointestinal issues like gas, bloating, cramping and irritable bowel, which is likely caused by these sugars and carbohydrates. A low FODMAP diet is great for correcting dysbiosis, mild SIBO (for those who tolerate grains, starch, fiber and sucrose), underweight clients, vegans and vegetarians, and as a transitionary diet from more restrictive diets once food tolerances have increased.

The Specific Carbohydrate Diet (SCD) was founded in the 1950's by Dr Sidney Valentine Haas who worked with coeliac disease and inflammatory bowel disease (IBD) sufferers. It was later developed further by Elaine Gottschall, whose daughter put her ulcerative colitis (UC) into remission using this diet. It looks and feels very similar to the low-carb diets, and dairy is avoided as well. It can work well as it focuses on limiting carbs which will help to stabilize blood sugar levels, as well as help with repairing the gut (to heal from leaky gut).

The Gut and Psychology Syndrome Diet (GAPS) was developed by Dr Natasha Campbell-McBride, and is largely based on SCD, with a few modifications for those with intestinal and neurological issues. GAPS is also called the monosaccharide (single sugar) diet. It is based on consuming a diet free of foods that contain disaccharides or polysaccharides, more complex sugars and carbohydrates, such as those in all grains, most beans, and most sweeteners. These complex sugars feed harmful bacteria in the small intestine that prevent its repair or proper function. It is therefore free of gains, starchy vegetables, legumes and most sweeteners. This diet is low-carb, and is done is stages. It can help to heal leaky gut and reduce inflammation, and is great for people who have many food sensitivities. The downside is that it can be very restrictive and depending on the person, it can be very challenging to adhere to.

The Mediterranean Diet is a very popular dietary approach, and rightly so. This diet has its origin from the island of Pantelleria in the Sicilian region of Italy. It focuses on eating the way that the people in the Mediterranean traditionally ate. There has been a lot of research done on this diet, and the diet is helpful in improving the health of people with certain conditions, like heart disease and cancer. People with non-autoimmune hypothyroid (underactive thyroid not caused by Hashimoto's Thyroiditis) will likely do well on this diet. The diet consists mostly of plant-based food and is relatively low in animal foods. The focus is on whole, unprocessed foods. Each meal includes vegetables, fruits and grains, while red meat, butter and processed foods are generally avoided.

Pulling it all together

After optimizing your thyroid hormone replacements, what you eat is the next most important thing to change. We have reviewed the mainstream diets so that you can understand what has worked for others, which ones you can consider. Avoid the inflammatory foods until your antibody markers have reduced. Remember that with Hashi's, you are focused on healing the autoimmune triggers that cause your immune system to attack your thyroid. There is no one-size-fits-all diet (as a way of eating). Other medical conditions will have an influence on how you approach your meals. The important thing is to understand what works for you, and creating a meal plan that you can enjoy while still nourishing your body.

Action Steps

1. **Start with going gluten-free.**

   There are great alternatives to replace gluten in recipes, like almond and coconut flours for baking. Be careful of packaged gluten-free products, as these often contain soy and high amounts of sugar.

2. **Replace dairy with non-dairy alternatives.**

   Milk is a staple for many, and luckily there are many alternatives to milk that you can start using for your drinks, cooking and baking. With beverages like coffee and tea you may need to experiment to find which options you like. Here are the alternatives to milk: coconut milk, almond milk or cashew milk. Rice milk is not an option, as it is derived from rice, an ingredient which we want to avoid as it is a grain.

   Almond milk and cashew milk are easy to make at home, and it is much healthier than store-bought almond milk. Many store-bought almond milks contain carrageenan, a known toxin, as well as guar gum as a stabilizer.

   For cheese and yoghurt alternatives, I recommend you consider dairy-free coconut yoghurt, vegan yoghurt and vegan "cheese".

3. **Replace vegetable and seed oils with healthy oils.**

   Seed and vegetable oils, like grapeseed, canola and sunflower oil, are inflammatory. If you have any of these oils in your kitchen, please throw them out or donate them. I always have a bottle of extra-virgin olive oil, organic coconut oil and avocado oil in my kitchen. Coconut oil is great for frying, while olive oil is fantastic to use over salads as a dressing, and avocado or olive oil is perfect for making roasted vegetables! Walnut oil or macadamia nut oil are also great to have available. You can also use free-range beef or duck lard for sealing meats and poultry dishes.

4. **Add healthy fats to your daily food intake.**

   Healthy fats are vital for your hormones and your thyroid, not to mention that they help to keep you fuller for longer! Here are some suggestions to include healthy fats in your diet: avocado, coconut oil, MCT oil (which is extracted from coconut oil), olive oil and nuts (try to avoid cashews as these are high in omega-6 fats) and seeds. Need some inspiration? Eat half an avocado with breakfast or with your salad, drizzle a teaspoon of olive oil over your salad, and you can add MCT oil to a smoothie.

5. **Replace sugar and sweeteners with healthier alternatives.**

   If you have a sweet tooth, it can be hard to cut out sugar immediately. I have done it, and you can too! However, if letting go of the sugar in your coffee and tea is too much too soon, I recommended that you replace sugar with healthier alternatives. A word of warning: not all sweeteners are created equally! Avoid artificial sweeteners, and rather use any of these options for your refreshments and in baking, keeping in mind that if you are going to follow a diet protocol like Paleo or AIP, some of these may not be allowed: raw honey, xylitol, stevia, erythritol, coconut sugar, agave syrup and dates.

   If you are using xylitol, just be careful of your intake. Too much xylitol can cause tummy discomfort and diarrhea. Stevia is a natural sugar that comes from the Stevia rebaudiana plant and is about 100 times sweeter than sugar! Many people don't like the taste of xylitol, while others don't like the taste of stevia. You need to test them and decide which alternative you prefer if you are considering using them. Erythritol is absorbed quickly in the small intestine and gets out of your body quickly through urine. This is a good alternative to use for people who struggle with blood sugar levels, as erythritol has no effect on glucose or insulin levels. Also, you can use it the same way as you use sugar, but in baked foods it may have different taste or consistency.

I have found that different ingredients work best for different things. I like to add a teaspoon tip of raw organic honey to my tea. For coffee, I have been able to cut out sugar completely. For smoothies, dates and bananas are delicious! For baking, I use xylitol, honey, bananas or dates. I haven't used erythritol much at the time of writing the book, so I can't comment on this product.

6. **Clean out spices that contains gluten and sugar.**

   Many of the combination bottles of spices (for example chicken spice) contain gluten (often in the form of breadcrumbs) and sugar. Read every spice and herb bottle that you have and remove it if it contains gluten and sugar.

7. **Replace soy sauce with coconut aminos.**

   Coconut aminos are a great alternative for soy sauce, especially if you like stir-fries. Look at your health shop for coconut aminos.

8. **Replace coffee with other healthier beverages.**

   There two big problems with coffee. First, there are a large quantity of chemicals in coffee. Second, a mold toxin called ochratoxin (which belongs to the group of fungal toxins called mycotoxins) is commonly found in coffee, which forms from how the coffee beans are stored. Some countries have set limits for ochratoxin that may be present, however, for many countries there are no set limits. The challenge comes when a batch of coffee beans that are over the limit are sold to countries with no limits. While roasting the coffee beans kills the mold, it doesn't remove the mold toxin. The best option for your health is to cut out coffee entirely. Consider herbal tea and chicory as a replacement for coffee.

9. **Drink a fresh (ideally cold-pressed) juice every day.**

Juicing is a great way to boost your nutrient intake without having to overload the gut. If you have a blender (like a Nutribullet™ or Vitamix™), you can make a blend of a selection of fruits and vegetables together which you can enjoy. The only holdback on a blended juice is that there is still a large amount of both insoluble and soluble fiber which can be heavy on the digestive tract.

If you have a juicer (I recommend a masticating or a triturating juicer), you remove the insoluble fiber while keeping all the nutrients and soluble fiber. Once you have juiced the fruit and vegetables, you can then blend in additional items such as avocado, banana, hemp seed, mixed seeds or berries (which provides provide amazing nutrients and insoluble fiber).

At this point in time, I don't want you to go on a juice-only program. It can be too extreme and stressful on your body. The goal for this step is to add just one juice drink to your day, either as a meal replacement or a healthy snack.

10. Create your new breakfast for the week and breakout breakfasts for the weekend.

Making changes to your diet is often the most important lifestyle change you can make, and it can also be the most daunting. So, let's do it slowly, starting with breakfast. The approach that I like and recommend is to decide on a breakfast that will work for you during the week, and to have breakout breakfasts for the weekend. The idea is to decide on one breakfast and eat it every day. Make it predicable and easy. Research for breakfast ideas that you like and that are free from gluten, dairy, sugar, soy, legumes and nightshades. Breakfast should nourish your body and your soul, as it is the first meal of the day!

11. Plan your lunch for the week.

Again, the idea here is to remove the stress from the "what's for lunch?" question. Search for three lunches that you like, and then eat one option for two days, then rotate it with another lunch for the next two days. Find a lunch that will fit your lifestyle. If you are on the road a lot, a homemade cold-pressed juice you prepared in the morning is ideal, while if you are office-based, a salad may be your best choice! Keep it simple and easy. If you plan what you have for lunch, you remove the stress of decisions and the temptation of eating at the company canteen or indulging in junk food. Look for some recipes and ideas that are free from gluten, dairy, sugar, soy, legumes and nightshades.

12. **Plan your healthy snacks.**

    Be ready with healthy snacks for those in-between meal snack pangs. A few ideas to get you started are fresh fruit, vegetable crudités, hard-boiled eggs or a handful of raw nuts and seeds.

13. **Plan your dinners for the week.**

    The last meal option we want to change is dinner. After a busy day at work, worrying about what to make for dinner should be the last thing on your mind. Plan out your dinner meals for the week, and before the week starts, ensure your pantry and fridge are well stocked with all the ingredients you like and need. If you can, make a meal or two on the weekend and freeze them. For those very busy days, you can then just remove the meal it from the freezer, add a salad and some veggies and you are good to go! Planning is the key here. When you plan, you reduce your stress and dinner anxiety, as well as make sure you are not tempted to revert to store-bought convenience foods or take-outs. As a bonus, try to incorporate turmeric, ginger and cinnamon, as these herbs are anti-inflammatory.

14. **Add fermented foods and/or beverages to your weekly meal plan.**

    Fermented foods are loaded with beneficial bacteria for your gut, and are good for your liver too! Sauerkraut and kombucha are good ideas to start with. Other options include fermented coconut yoghurt, fermented coconut water, and kimchi. Health shops also stock home-made kombucha kits, should you want to make your own. Remember to keep fermented foods in the refrigerator. If you have SIBO, skip this step as the fermented foods may exacerbate your symptoms.

15. **Research restaurants in your area for eat-out meals.**

    There will be times that you are going to go out for a meal at a restaurant. Take some time to research the restaurants in your area at home and at work and look at their menus. Many restaurants have their menus available on their websites. Make a list of the restaurants that offer meals that you can enjoy and make a list of the restaurant and the meals available. Now, when you are going to a restaurant, you know exactly which ones you can go to and which menu items you can order!

16. **Make your own bone broth.**

    Most commercial beef, chicken or vegetable stock contains gluten. You can make your own bone broth. The benefit of making your own is that you make sure you use bones from grass-fed beef or free-range chicken, and that the broth it is slowly cooked (anything between 12 to 24 hours) to extract all the nutrition. Bone broth also contains gelatin that helps to heal the gut lining.

17. **Check for any other food intolerances or allergies if you are still experiencing symptoms.**

    If you have removed gluten, grains, dairy, soy and nightshades from your diet and your thyroid hormone therapy is optimized, it may be time to talk to your doctor about testing for any other allergies or food intolerances. It is a process of elimination, and while food intolerances or allergies may not be the culprit, you need to rule this out before continuing with the next step:

checking for heavy metal toxicity and treatment with LDN (low dose naltrexone).

18. **Consult with a dietician or nutritionist**

The right dietician or nutritionist can be a great source of information and support to help you determine the best dietary approach for you.

CHAPTER 10: PILLAR 5 - SLEEP

Sleep has been the focus of many research studies recently, and specifically how sleep is important for high and sustainable performance at work. The impact of sleep on health has also gained a lot of attention in recent years, and how sleep, or specifically the lack of sleep, has an impact on general health, mental performance and the body's ability to maintain a healthy weight. Sleep is vital for our wellbeing: it helps with many aspects in our waking lives, it helps our ability to control body weight, it aids in regulating emotions and it bolsters our immune system. It also enhances memory and mental clarity, improves athletic performance, improves immune function and increases stress tolerance. Insufficient sleep, which is less than seven to eight hours a night, shortens your life expectancy, and raises the risk for type 2 diabetes, cardiovascular disease and high blood pressure.

I have struggled for many years with getting a good night's sleep. When I have been in a state of good health, I would be able to go to sleep in an instant and wake up eight hours later feeling refreshed and ready for the day. But when my Hashi's flared up, sleep has been the one thing that was severely impacted. First, I felt a level of exhaustion that just never went away, no matter how much I slept during the day, during the night or even over weekends. When I finally fell asleep, it would be for a short period, and I would wake up at midnight or just thereafter, feeling so tired, but unable to fall asleep again. It was a vicious cycle – the more sleep I wanted, the more exhausted I got, the more stressed I got about not being able to sleep, and the less I could sleep!

In this section we are doing to talk about the zzzz's, and what you can do to get a good night's sleep, starting with the basics on what you can do to set you up for a good night's sleep.

The link between sleep and body weight

A lack of sleep can make you fat. Really. How does that work?

Researchers found that a lack of sleep changes the chemicals in the brain that affect appetite and energy levels. So, when you are sleep deprived and you see junk food, your brain's ability to resist is impaired and the drive for junk food is higher!

Did you know that sleep and the hunger hormones work together? The two hunger hormones I am referring to are leptin and ghrelin. When you don't get enough sleep, leptin (which suppresses appetite) goes down, while ghrelin (which stimulates appetite) goes up! You wake up in the middle of the night with cravings!

So not sleeping enough really can make you fat. This is not what we want. So let's have a look at what we can do to make sure we get enough restorative and energizing sleep.

Train your body to sleep

Getting into a routine is one of the best and easiest things you can do to help train your body to sleep. It may take time for your body to adjust to your new sleep routine. Here are my top tips to get you sleeping well again.

Go to bed at the same time and aim to wake up at the same time every day, including weekends. You can determine your go-to-bed time by looking at when you want to wake and then count backwards eight hours to determine what time you need to get into bed.

Here's an example of how I worked out my go-to-sleep time: I need to get up at 05h15, so my go-to-sleep time is eight hours earlier, at 21h15. I make sure that I switch off the light at 21h15. I also like some time to read before I sleep, so I aim to get into bed at 21h00.

You will also see that you need to go to sleep and wake up at the same time EVERY DAY. It means that you go to sleep and wake up the same time over weekends as well, when you are on holiday, or on the days that you may not have anything else to do. The idea is to make your go-to-sleep time a habit.

What about when you are going out – say to movies or an event? No problem, as of course we have lives to live! The idea is that for most of the time, you go to sleep at the same time and wake up at the same time.

I saw a huge positive impact in my health when I started to implement a set sleep-time and a set wake-up time. After a couple of days, I didn't need an alarm to wake me up anymore. I was waking up naturally just before my alarm went off. Now that is a good feeling!

If you wake up during in the night, don't get up or look at your phone. When you get up, you are likely to switch on a light or two, go and watch television or do something on your computer. If you do this, you will signal to your brain that it is time to wake up and get to work, and it will make you even less likely to get back to sleep. Also, never look at your phone. The blue light that comes from your phone screen signals the brain to wake up.

Should you wake up during in the night, force yourself to stay in bed. You need to get your body used to sleeping when you want it to sleep. If you really can't get back to sleep, read a boring book, a real book using a small book-reading light, and not on your phone or tablet which emits blue light.

Create your own go-to-bed routine. Develop your own wind-down routine and do it every night. When you start your routine, this will signal your body to wind down and get ready for sleep. Here are some ideas on what you can do to create your own wind-down routine: stop working on your computer (including checking social media, emails or watching programs). Dim the lights in the house to trigger an increase in melatonin levels, enjoy a cup of tea, write in a journal to reflect on your day or things you are grateful for, take a hot bath or shower. Consider listening to calming music, or do a relaxing or sleep meditation, read something you enjoy (like a novel) or gaze at the moon and stars.

Drink magnesium before you go to sleep. Magnesium is not toxic (it is safe up to 800 mg a day), it's cheap and easy to find. There are seven different forms of magnesium, so it may be worthwhile to find the form that works for you. Take magnesium before you go to bed and make it part of your daily sleep routine.

What you do in the day affects your sleep. If you are running around all day, with stressor after stressor after stressor, it may be very difficult for your body to just switch off and go to sleep. Your nervous system has been working hard and it can't slow down and shut down. Aim to get outside during the day, as sunshine is good for you and acts like a mood-booster. Exercise can also help, but avoid exercising late at night as your body may struggle to relax and fall asleep.

Avoid alcohol. While you think you may enjoy a glass of wine with your evening meal, the alcohol can lead to poor quality sleep.

Eat your dinner earlier. Dinner is often the main meal for people, and a big meal later in the evening can cause you to be awake. Eating pushes up the body's core temperature as your body goes to work to digest the food, which doesn't help if you want your body to wind down for sleeping. If possible, try to make lunch your main meal of the day, and enjoy a light dinner at around 18h00.

Have your last cup of coffee or black tea by latest 2 o'clock in the afternoon, or even better, avoid coffee completely. The caffeine in coffee, black and green tea is a stimulant which will help keep you awake.

If you are hungry before bedtime, have a banana or some unsalted walnuts or almonds. Bananas are an excellent source of magnesium and potassium (which helps to relax over-stressed muscles), while unsalted nuts like walnuts are a good source of tryptophan (an amino acid which helps boost melatonin). Almonds are also rich in muscle-relaxing magnesium.

Create a restful environment

Your sleep environment can impact your quality of sleep. When you look at your bedroom, it should be a haven of peace, tranquility and calm. Here are my tips to help you create a relaxing and calm room:

- Remove the television. A television emits blue light, which hampers your body's ability to create melatonin.
- Change to light-colored bed linen that reflects the light instead of absorbing it. Also, get the best quality linen you can afford – the higher the cotton content and thread count, the better, as cotton keeps you cool and dry.

- Keep your room dark when you go to sleep. Any light that comes through from outside can impact your ability to sleep.
- Keep your room cool, between 15 degrees Celsius and 18 degrees Celsius. In summer you can achieve this by keeping your curtains drawn during the day to block out the sun. Later in the evening, open the windows to let in a breeze and use a fan throughout the night if necessary.
- Keep your room clean and clutter-free. Vacuum your mattress regularly to clean it of dust mites and microscopic creatures, and wash your bed linen weekly on a cycle of at least 60 degrees Celsius.
- Add a plant to your room. Not only can it help with cleaning the air, it can also give off sedative scents. Consider jasmine, gardenia, aloe vera and lavender plants.

Can you take a nap when you are tired?

Exhaustion is a debilitating symptom when you experience an autoimmune flare-up. When this happens, I recommend that you listen to your body and sleep when you need to. When I experience flare-ups, I sleep a lot, even during the day. But when we talk about taking a nap, I am not referring to when you are having a flare-up. This is about when you are struggling to fall asleep at night.

Napping is a complex issue, and there are no simple answers on whether nor not it is good for you to take a nap. You can determine whether it is good for you by checking if taking a nap in the afternoon is impacting your ability to fall asleep at night. Dr Lawrence Epstein stated that there are good naps and bad naps. "Bad naps" are when you take a nap due to chronic insomnia. It is often when people get less than 6 hours of sleep at night, which leads to feeling sleepy during the day. When people then take a nap, and often a long one, it perpetuates the cycle of nigh time insomnia and daytime sleepiness.

If you are experiencing a short-term issue that impacts your sleep, for example from a sick child, a nap can help you recover during the day. Naps can also help to refresh the brain for the work-demands of the afternoon. The trick is to keep the nap between 15 to 20 minutes, and nap just after lunch.

Other things that impact sleep

If you have done everything you can to create quality sleep and you are still not able to sleep, you need to start investigating other reasons why you are unable to sleep. These include a Hashi's flareup, underlying medical conditions or even other over-the-counter or prescription medication you may be taking. Let's look at each of these in more detail.

- **Look at your medicine cabinet**. If you are struggling with getting quality sleep, it may be worthwhile to have a look at what other medications you are taking. Prescription drugs can contribute to your inability to sleep, as several medications can interfere with sleep, according to Dr Lawrence Epstein. Sleeping pills are not recommended for long-term use, as they can become less effective over time. Prescription medications and many over-the-counter decongestants and weight loss products contain stimulants that can impact your ability to sleep.

- **Check for underlying medical conditions**. There might also be other reasons why you may be struggling to fall asleep and stay asleep. First, if you experience an urge to move your legs, snoring or a burning pain in your stomach, chest or throat, see your doctor for an evaluation. You may have restless legs syndrome, sleep apnea or gastroesophageal reflux disease (GERD). Psychological problems like depression and anxiety, or traumatic experiences can also impact your sleep. If you and your doctor suspect a sleep disorder such as narcolepsy, periodic limb movement disorder, sleep apnea or one of the parasomnias, you may need to go for formal sleep testing at a sleep laboratory.

Action Steps

1. **Create a bed-time routine.**

   Quality sleep is vital for your health! Create your bed-time routine, which can include activities like dimming the lights, taking a relaxing bath with essential oils, meditation, reflecting on the day, enjoying a cup of chamomile tea, reading for 15 minutes or even moon gazing! If you are feeling hungry at bedtime, eat a banana or some unsalted walnuts or almonds. Remember to drink your magnesium!

2. **Go to bed at the same time every night.**

   The idea is to get 7 to 8 hours of quality sleep, and to train your body and brain to do it. Start with deciding what time you need to get up in the morning before work, and then count backwards by 8 hours. This is the time that you need to be in bed and switch off the light. Now, go to bed at the same time every night. It may be difficult at first but stick with it. Even over weekends, aim to keep the same bedtime and wake-up time.

3. **Change your bedroom into a sleep haven.**

   Your bedroom should be a serene space to encourage sleep. Here are a few ideas to help you change it to a sleep haven: remove the TV if you have one, buy light colored bed linen, use essential oils as soft smells help reduce stress (lavender, rose, chamomile, ylang ylang are all great options), use an air diffuser or bring in a beautiful plant to help purify the air. You can also consider aroma therapy candles to create soft smells and it is romantic too!

4. **Review your prescription medications.**

   Some medications may interfere with your sleep. If you suspect this may be the case, consult with your doctor about options and alternatives.

5. **Check for underlying medical conditions.**

   If you suspect that an underlying medical condition may be the cause of your sleep problems, consult with your doctor about diagnosis and treatment options.

CHAPTER 11: PILLAR 6 - STRESS

Stress and managing stress are two of the topics that we all know something about, and we know what we should be doing, and yet we are not doing it! We are somehow coping with the demands of life, but we don't always acknowledge the impact that stress has on our bodies. Even more, we underestimate the impact of stress on our health.

Stress impacts the entire body – including the immune system. Since the inflammation in the body is the core of the problem when you have Hashi's, it is important to understand how stress impacts not just the body, but also the immune system and its role in inflammation. Only by understanding this impact can we then take action to mitigate the impact of stress, calm our immune systems and take our health back.

First, let's start by understanding the impact of stress on the body, how stress impacts the immune system, and then we are going to look at the various tools at your disposal to mitigate the impact of stress. Stress is not going to go away, so we need to know what to do when stress starts to affect us. There are two different types of stressors: sudden stress and chronic stress. Let's start with a simplistic yet important overview of what happens when we are suddenly stressed, and then what happens when we are chronically stressed.

The body's response to stress

When we talk about the body's response to stress, Professor Robert Sapolsky (specialist in neuroscience in the course *The Great Courses: Stress and the Body*) from Stanford University explained it well. The body seeks homeostasis – to always be in balance with the ideal pressure, temperature, level of glucose in the bloodstream and so on. Sapolsky defines stress as anything that disrupts the homeostatic balance of the body. With that in mind, we can start to understand the impact of stress on the body. Also, you can read his book *Why Zebras Don't Get Ulcers* which will have a lot more detail that what I provide here.

The body has a built-in stress-response system. It works great for when we are suddenly faced with a stressor – this is the response that is designed to save your life. When you are knocked off your homeostatic balance, the short-term physical crisis leads to the stress-response. Take, for example, if you are suddenly attacked by a lion. You are facing a life-threatening event and your body is reacting accordingly by turning the stress response on.

When you are suddenly stressed, you need energy quickly to be able to act. This energy required is needed rapidly, and so the body will go and get the energy that is currently in your system, which is the energy that is already available in the bloodstream, namely glucose. The energy that is stored away in the fat cells is not touched, as it will take too long to get it out. Now, you want to get the available glucose as fast as possible to the muscles. To help get it there faster, your heart rate increases, your breathing increases, and your blood pressure increases. Another thing that happens during this stress-response is that all the long-term building projects are paused: digestion, growth and reproduction, tissue repair, to name a few. The body also kicks the immune system into gear in anticipation of possible injury or infection – to clot the blood or fight the infection. Stress also blunts pain perception so that when you are injured, you don't feel it. All these things happen in preparation to help you fight or run. Stress hormones are released into your brain, and with the increased glucose and oxygen, short-term memory is enhanced so that you are alert and focused.

These are all great actions the body does to deal with an emergency. But what happens with chronic stress? Every day is an emergency, but it is usually not the real "a-lion-is-going-to-eat-me" emergency, but more psychological reasons, like worry. The stress-response is now being switched on all the time. With chronic stress, you turn off growth, healing, reproduction, digestion and it also wears out the body, as all the maintenance and building projects in the body are paused.

The two systems

There are two systems in the body that responds to stress: the nervous system and the hormonal system.

First, let's talk about the nervous system. The brain heads up the nervous system and is all about voluntary movement (which is called the voluntary nervous system). It is when you decide to do something, and your brain gets your body to do it. There is also a part of the nervous system which does things automatically, like blushing, breathing and goose bumps. This part of the nervous system is called the autonomic nervous system. The autonomic nervous system has two halves to it: the one half is called the sympathetic nervous system and the other half is called the parasympathetic system.

The first half, the sympathetic nervous system, kicks into action when "all hell breaks loose" and it is all about the flight-or-fight response. The other half, the parasympathetic nervous system, does the exact opposite: it mediates calmness and vegetative function. For the most part, they work in opposition.

Stress and the stress response are all about turning on the sympathetic nervous system to an extremely severe extent while turning the parasympathetic nervous system off. What regulates this switching on of the sympathetic nervous system? Nothing other than the brain.

Looking conceptually at the brain, there are three components to it: the reptilian brain, the limbic brain and the cortex. These three components of the brain are also referred to as the triune brain. The reptilian brain is the oldest part of the brain, and this does all the regulatory stuff, like when you are feeling cold, the brain signals to the muscles to shiver to generate heat. The second layer is the limbic brain. This system is all about the emotions that mammals have – joy, anger, frustration, pleasure, lust and rage, to name a few. The third layer is the cortex, which is the most recent evolvement of the brain. The functionality of the cortex includes abstract reasoning, long term memory, and decision-making, to name a few.

One of the interesting concepts that Professor Sapolsky explains is that any part of the triune brain can turn on the stress-response. If you are hurt, your reptilian brain turns on the stress-response; if you are threatened by someone, your limbic brain turns on the stress-response; and if you think about global warming and incurable diseases and that you might die at any point in time, your cortex can turn on the stress response!

So even our thoughts can cause the limbic and reptilian brain to turn on the stress response AS IF you are being attacked and AS IF you are hurt and are bleeding!

Now, let's review the second system, the hormonal system. The hormones come from glands and impact various parts of the body. When you are stressed and the brain activates the stress response, the brain (and specifically the hypothalamus) releases hormones that inform the pituitary gland which hormones to release in order to instruct a variety of glands to release other hormones.

The brain instructs the adrenal glands to secrete an important hormone - glucocorticoids (also known as hydrocortisone or cortisol). There are other hormones that are also increased in the stress response, including prolactin, glucagon and beta-endorphins. Then there are the hormones that the parasympathetic nervous system inhibits or stops during the stress response, and those include growth hormone, insulin, and the reproductive hormones.

Now that we understand how the stress response works, we can continue with how stress impacts your metabolism, your gut, your immune system and your thyroid. It's almost like everything is falling apart when we are stressed! And it does fall apart when we are stressed. It's not a pretty picture, and once we know what happens to our bodies when we are stressed, we can then take action to mitigate the impact of stress on our bodies and our health.

Stress and your metabolism

So, what happens with your metabolism when you are suddenly stressed?

When we eat food, the body breaks down the food: protein into amino acids, fat into fatty acids and glycerol, and carbohydrates into glucose. These then enter the bloodstream, and what is not used by the cells is stored away.

The body cannot store these excess nutrients in the form that is in the blood stream, so it needs to convert it back in its complex forms: amino acids are stored as protein, simple sugars are grouped and stored as glycogen, and the fatty acids and glycerol are stored as fat.

The pivotal hormone responsible for this change process is insulin. Think about insulin as the hormone of plenty – when there are plenty nutrients, insulin is secreted by the pancreas.

Now think about what you just read. Suddenly stress is causing your body to stop storing nutrients and rather flush your body with energy so that you can fight or run. What happens with your metabolism when you have chronic stress? Unfortunately, there is a lot of potential for problems.

With chronic stress, you move between the two systems: storing energy and releasing energy. You store away energy, and then you release it. Then you store it, then you release it. You store it, you release it. You get the picture. But all this in-and-out energy processing comes at a price. The storage and release process isn't 100 percent efficient anymore – there is a cost to this constant processing!

You get stressed, get over it, get stressed, get over it. With each stress response you are releasing sugar into the blood stream, and then you want to store it again, meaning that there are huge highs and lows in the blood sugar levels, and keeping the blood sugar levels stable becomes very challenging. Your risk to develop type 2 diabetes increases. As Professor Sapolsky explains, the body wants to store the excess nutrients, but due to a sedentary lifestyle and eating too much junk food, the fat cells have stored what they can and are full. This is a big problem. What to do now?

So when you are stressed, your body secretes glucocorticoids (cortisol), epinephrine (adrenalin) and glucagon (hormone to get energy from storage) to block insulin and mobilize energy. Now, the brain steps in and "instructs" the fat cells to ignore the insulin to make sure that no nutrients are stored - just in case the pancreas might still be secreting any insulin. Now you become resistant to insulin. The body is not responding or "listening" to insulin anymore. This is moving you towards developing insulin-resistant diabetes. The problem is that insulin resistance can lead to hyperglycemia, then cardiovascular damage, which increases your risk of metabolic disease.

Stress and your gut

What does stress do your appetite? And more so, what does stress do your digestive tract? Remember that what you eat can lead to "leaky gut"? In this section, we will see what the impact of stress is on the gut.

Let's start with the first component: what stress does to your appetite. Some people eat more, and some people eat less. You probably know which group you fall into. I know I fall into the first group; I definitely eat more! And I then crave all the wrong foods: starchy, fatty and sugary foods!

The brain is the reason why we eat more when we are stressed. When you experience stress, the brain secretes a particular (hypothalamic) hormone, telling the pituitary gland to secrete a hormone which tells the adrenal glands to secrete glucocorticoids (cortisol). Remember that this is the flight-or-fight hormone, and that your body's stress response is to get energy to the muscles. So while cortisol helps to shut down insulin, it also stimulates the appetite so that you can replace the energy after you have been running for your life! As soon as the stress is over, and you are now safe, it takes a few minutes for the glucocorticoids (cortisol) levels to return to normal, leaving you hungry. This is the recovery phase of the stress response.

Now think about what happens when you are chronically stressed. If you are dealing with so many stressful situations, like being stuck in traffic, being late for work, working for a horrible boss and hectic deadlines to name a few, you turn on the stress response every time! And for every time you turn it on, there is a recovery period for each event and your appetite increases for each stress-response! This is why so many people eat more during periods of stress! But when you eat more, you also crave those exact foods which are high in energy: bread, sugars and fatty foods! There is one good thing about eating carbohydrates when you are stressed: the carbohydrates are broken down into sugars, insulin increases, and it suppresses the release of glucocorticoids (cortisol). By eating you are literally decreasing your stress!

But where do the excess nutrients go now that you are eating because you are stressed? They must go somewhere. These nutrients are stored in the fat cells. There are two types of fat: the fat that ends up on your stomach (abdominal fat), and the fat that ends up on your bottom (gluteal fat). The abdominal fat is concerning, as it is dangerous. It releases inflammatory signals. It also is very close to your liver, which can lead to fatty liver. Another thing is that abdominal fat is pulling your spine forward. So overall, abdominal fat is just not good for you.

There is another thing that happens in the gut when we are stressed: the digestive system shuts down temporarily. You cannot waste energy on absorbing nutrients. You also need to get rid of whatever is in your colon that could weigh you down! Therefore, you need to go to the bathroom more often when you are suddenly stressed!

The problem with chronic stress is that your risk for gastrointestinal disorders increases. You are at higher risk to develop irritable bowel syndrome (IBS) and spastic colon.

Stress and your immune system

This is probably the most important part of stress that we need to know about: the impact of stress on the immune system. It is a complex field and we'll briefly review the impact of stress on the immune system.

When you are stressed, your body activates the immune system in anticipation of a possible injury or infection. The sympathetic nervous system and glucocorticoids (cortisol) to help activate the immune system. The glucocorticoids also kill some of the old immune cells, and the immune response will also take some of the circulating immune cells and rushes them to where the injury is. This is all good and necessary when injury is imminent!

But what does the research tell us about chronic stress and autoimmunity? The research is not strong on the fact that stress causes autoimmune diseases, but what is well known is that stress is a huge contributor to flare-ups once you have an autoimmune disease.

There is another element to chronic stress and the immune system that we need to know. Glucocorticoids (cortisol) also plays another role in the immune system, specifically during the recovery phase, and helps to get the immune system back to a normal level. Here is how it plays out in our bodies:

- Short-term stress, and the immune system is activated.
- More sustained stress, after enhancing immunity, the immune system is brought back to base line.
- Major league chronic stress suppresses the immune system as the glucocorticoids suppress the immune system below the base line, which can lead to immunosuppression.

This can explain when you have an autoimmune and inflammatory disease, why doctors prescribe synthetic glucocorticoids (cortical steroids). It is to help bring the over-activated immune system back to normal levels, and the names you may hear or be familiar with are hydrocortisone and prednisone.

Stress and pain

One of the symptoms of Hashi's is body pain, and stress and pain are unfortunately intertwined. Pain can be a stressor, and stress can also cause a change in how sensitive you are to pain. While in general the short-term stress response is good and the long-term stress response is bad, it doesn't always work this way with pain.

Pain is a strong signal to show when something is wrong. There are sensors everywhere in your body that respond when something is wrong. It sends signals to your brain to act, like taking your hand out of the fire. There is a model that explains how pain signaling works, called the Wall-Melzack model. But what we want to know is what the impact of stress is on pain.

First, stress numbs pain. This is called stress-induced analgesia, and it generally happens with the release of beta-endorphins. Let me explain with an example of what happened with me in karate many years ago. We had a training session practicing fighting techniques, and while we did our cool-down exercises, I noticed blood on my right foot. Then I noticed that the little toe's nail had been completely ripped off, sometime during the class. The intense exercise caused stress-induced analgesia, because I didn't even feel it! But 20 minutes later, I did! As I cooled down, the toe began to throb, and within minutes the pain was excruciating!

Second, pain can be exaggerated when you have sustained chronic stress, as the pain pathways become more sensitive because of the sustained stimulation. You become "depleted" of beta-endorphin (so much is produced to try and numb the pain that they just can't keep up with the demand), and instead of being able to shut down the pain, the pain comes back and keeps going. This exaggerated pain sensitivity is called hyperalgesia.

Stress and pain work together. If you are in pain, be careful that you don't increase the pain by being stressed about the pain. If you are experiencing this, focus on strategies to help reduce your stress so that your pain levels also decrease.

Stress and the thyroid gland

Stress has an impact on just about every system in the body, and because the body shuts down all the long-term systems in the body, the thyroid gland is impacted as well. In fact, the thyroid gland is not vital for your get-away response, and is therefore paused.

First, you experience stress and as part of the stress response, the brain (specifically the hypothalamus) releases hormones that inform the pituitary gland which hormones to release to instruct a variety of glands to release other hormones. There are also hormones which are slowed down as certain systems are not critical during the flight-or-fight response, and the thyroid hormones are included in this group. So the thyroid gland then receives the message to produce less thyroid hormones.

Remember in Chapter 3 we reviewed the conversion of the inactive hormone T4 to the active hormone T3? When you are stressed, the enzymes that are supposed to convert T4 hormones to the active T3 hormones are impacted, and the T4 hormones are now converted to the useless reverse T3 hormone. Therefore, there are even less active T3 hormones available for the body to use. This is why I support testing for reverse T3 when you are experiencing high levels of stress.

Chronic stress is bad for us. There is no other way to say it. It puts a huge toll on our bodies, and it adds to the problem of inflammation. The problem is that we also cannot quit our jobs and go and sit in a cave and meditate for the rest of our lives. We need to learn tools and strategies on how we can decrease the body's stress response, and what we can do to limit the damaging impacts of chronic stress on our health.

Strategies to mitigate the impact of stress

Robert Epstein, a Harvard-trained psychologist, recommends that the most effective way to deal with stress is to sidestep potential stressors before they happen. It sounds easy, but it is not. In this section, we will look at what you can do to limit stress before it starts, and then, what you can do if you are already stressed. There are ten strategies and tools that I would like to share with you. We will cover each strategy briefly, and then you can decide which strategy will fit with your lifestyle and budget. If you are struggling to address the stress, or experience depression or anxiety, please seek medical advice.

Here are the ten stress-busting strategies:

Fight stress before it starts	**Reduce stress when you are stressed**
1. Clear your diary 2. Plan your week 3. Grab the good stuff 4. Let it go 5. Good enough is good enough	6. Get moving 7. Create moments of mindfulness 8. Use pure essential oils 9. Infrared sauna therapy 10. Become un-busy

Tool 1: Clear out the diary.

Let's be honest here. We are all busy. We have busy lives, with demanding schedules and endless to-do lists. Societal pressure almost demands that we need to be busy, and if you are not, you are made to feel lazy and guilty. Self-care is not high on the list, and for many of us, it is not even on the list at all!

There is one thing that we must do before we do anything else: we must have time to rest and recover, especially when you have a Hashi's flare up! You must become selfish with your time so that you can rest and recover. Before you do anything, clear up your time. Remove, reduce, automate, delegate, outsource and improve - these are your strategies.

Here are few suggestions:

- **What can you say "No" to?** Learn to love the word "no". Boundaries are wonderful. Say no to people who want some of your time and you don't have the energy to deal with them. Say no to those meetings that you don't need to attend. Say no to being on the club committee, unless it is something that you really want to do and that you enjoy doing.
- **What can you remove?** Another suggestion is to get rid of clutter. Clutter, physical and mental, takes up space and can cause stress. Adopt a minimalist approach to your home. By making physical space, you also create mental space. How about the people who stress you out? If you have people in your life who constantly take and never give, who just keep on complaining and who just

demand from you all the time, it is time to cut the ties. This does not only apply to people you know, but also to family. It can be very difficult to avoid family, but for your own sanity and peace, you must find a way to limit your time with them.

- **What can you automate?** Change your physical mail delivery to electronic delivery and put a rule in place in your email software to place it in a dedicated folder. Put a timer on the sprinkler system for the garden. Find ways to automate as much of what can be automated.
- **What can you delegate or outsource?** Can someone else attend the meeting in your place? Can you outsource the cleaning of your house? If you don't like preparing meals, can you outsource meal preparation to your partner, kids or even a delivery service?
- **What can you improve?** Can you fix the broken watch or get it fixed?

Tool 2: Plan your week

Making decisions is energy-draining. Research has found that your brain has a limited amount of energy available to make decisions. When you use up this limited amount of energy, it can lead to something called decision fatigue. Think about a time that you had to go shopping. After walking from shop to shop, hours later, you may buy that pair of shoes that don't actually fit you well at all. This is decision fatigue.

We want to try and limit the number of decisions we must make each day and save the energy for the really important things in our lives and at work. So, here are two tools that you can employ to limit decision fatigue and avoid the stress that comes with it.

- **Plan the activities**. Sit down over the weekend and plan your week. Put all the activities that you need to do in your calendar. This will include visits to the gym, walks in the park, visits to the dentist, kids' activities, time with friends, shopping, sporting activities, meetings with clients. Add in preparation time for your meetings or presentations. You get the idea. Also block out time to do focused work, a time to think or even daydream, and a time to relax (that all-important me-time). What gets scheduled, gets done.
- **Plan your meals**. Planning your week also includes planning your meals. One of the easiest strategies I found is to have the same meal for breakfast and the same meal for lunch. Decide what you are going to have for dinner in the upcoming week. Then, do all the shopping on a Saturday or Sunday. Last minute visits to the grocery store can create stress, as it puts pressure on your time. If a food delivery service is an option, you can have your food delivered to you. There are also services available to have the raw ingredients delivered with a recipe, and all you must do is make the meal. Just a word of caution here. Avoid the prepacked frozen food that is available from the grocery store. These are often filled with ingredients that are not good for you, and can add to the load on your body, especially if you have Hashi's and you are trying to avoid certain foods that add to inflammation.

- **Implement Self-Care Sundays**. Part of your planning is to dedicate a day in the week to take care of yourself. For many people, including myself, this day is on a Sunday. This is the day that you don't work, and you focus on doing activities that you like, that give you energy and maybe even sparks a little creativity! This is your recharge day, and I like to call it Self-care Sunday. Many people will tell you to have a tech-free day, but I find that advice rather naïve. I love to play music that I enjoy and gets me grooving from Spotify during the day, and when I get creative and stuck into my photography, I am working on my computer. So, it's not about having a tech-free day, it's about having a work-free day. If you feel lazy and tired, there is nothing wrong with binge-watching television and catching up on a series that you enjoy! Self-care Sundays are also a great reason to get outdoors and into nature. Go take a walk in a park, relax on the beach, or watch a sunset. The only requirement? Don't do work. Do anything and everything but work.

Tool 3: Grab the good stuff

Humans are inherently negative. We tend to notice and remember the bad things that happen during the day. Can we do anything to change this negative perception? Of course, we can.

At the end of each day, as part of your bed-time ritual, take five minutes to reflect on the day. Review what went well and what didn't. Then, write down three good things that happened to you, that you are grateful for, or that you enjoyed. Reflect on the importance of these three things. This exercise only takes a few minutes. Studies (by

Seligman et al.) showed that people who made this activity a habit, had increased levels of happiness and optimism! The next morning, have a quick review of the list you made the night before as you start your new day.

Pleasure is another tool we can look at. When pleasure is experienced, your body releases chemicals called endorphins, which help to counteract stress and improve your mood. Think about what makes you happy, or if you are in a place of stress right now, what used to make you happy. Play with a pet, listen to your favorite music, phone a friend, watch a comedic sitcom or movie or spend time outdoors.

Tool 4: Let it go

Often, we worry about and try to manage things that are out of our control, and this creates stress. Have a look at what you can and cannot control. You can only do something about what you can control. If you have no control over it, let it go. Consider the things you have very little or no control over: the weather, the traffic and other people are good examples. Let it go. The only things you can control are your own actions and reactions.

To illustrate the point, when my daughter was in Grade 5, at 11 years old, she was becoming anxious and stressed about the upcoming end-of-year exams. In the conversation we had, she said that she was worried about what the teacher might ask, and that she wouldn't be able to answer the questions. In talking about what is in her control and what is not, she realized that she had no control over what the teacher might ask in the exam. She did however, have control over how well she prepared for the exam. By realizing that, she focused her efforts and thoughts on what she could control – how she spent her time in preparation for the tests.

Tool 5: Good enough is good enough

The strive for perfection can place a huge amount of stress on a person. Replace "perfect" with "good enough". The pursuit of perfection can be very destructive, as the striving for perfection is often rooted in the fear of failure. By aiming to be perfect, you put so much pressure on yourself and that creates stress. Perfection is an impossible goal to achieve.

Dr. Brene Brown, a research professor and TEDx speaker, confirmed that perfection has a cost. She said *"Perfection is correlated with depression, anxiety, addiction, and life paralysis or missed opportunities. The fear of failing, making mistakes, not meeting people's expectations, and being criticized, keeps us outside of the arena where healthy competition and striving unfolds*". Stop worrying and adding to your stress over being perfect. Adopt a "good enough" attitude and let go of the rest.

Tool 6: Get moving

Exercise helps in many ways: it decreases your chances of cardiovascular disease, it also stimulates and helps to grow new neurons, and it helps to make you feel better. But if you are like me, it doesn't come easy, as a busy life and many demands all vie for your time. What can you do to get moving?

First, find something you enjoy. You will not stick to any exercise if you don't like it. Don't force yourself to go running when you hate running. Also, do look at what is not traditionally labelled as exercise. You also don't have to join a gym to exercise. How about dancing, playing indoor netball or cricket, to name a few. The thing that is important is to find something that you like doing!

Tool 7: Create moments of being mindful

When we are stressed, the fight or flight function of our bodies is on full alert. To counter that reaction, we should focus on activating the parasympathetic nervous system to calm down. Mindfulness helps to activate the parasympathetic system.

What is mindfulness? Mindfulness is simply a state of active, open attention on the present. You carefully observe your thoughts and feelings, without judging them. You simply acknowledge and accept your feelings, thoughts and bodily sensations. There are three avenues of mindfulness: meditation, mindful eating and mindful sleeping

- **Meditation.** There are a huge amount of resources available on meditation - books, podcasts, articles, research, and audio programs to name a few. There is good reason for this - meditation really does pack a powerhouse of benefits. It helps to reduce stress, reduce pain, improve your self-control and a healthier brain. There are different forms of meditation that you can explore, including mindfulness meditation, breath awareness meditation, body scan meditation, loving-kindness meditation, transcendental meditation and Kundalini yoga. Any meditation can help you cultivate positivity, energy and focus. If one style doesn't work for you, then try another until you and find the type of meditation that works for you.

- **Mindful eating.** Stop eating on the run. Mindful eating is based on the Buddhist concept of mindfulness: the process of bringing your mind to experience the present. Mindful eating is merely paying attention to the food you are eating while you are eating it - noticing the colors and smells, experiencing the textures and savoring the flavors of what you are putting into your mouth and gifting your body. A fast-growing body of research suggests that mindful eating could even help with weight issues. Now, this is not about meditating while you are eating, but simply putting all your attention on the food you are eating and removing distractions like cell phones and watching television shows.
- **Mindful sleeping.** While the topic of sleep is discussed separately in this book, the concept of mindful sleeping is what we'll talk about here. In an article in Psychology Today, Rubin Naiman Ph.D., said that a mindful approach to sleep must begin with looking at why we are so mindless about sleep. We just go about going to sleep, and it is here we have an opportunity to be mindful about sleep. To be more mindful about sleep, Naiman has a few suggestions:
    - Reduce the light at night and tune into your mind as the light turns into darkness. What are you seeing in the dark? What are you feeling?

- You know that weird space where you are between being awake and falling asleep? Become aware of that space.
- Become aware of your body as you fall asleep. Lie in your bed and observe your eyelids, your arms, your legs and your torso. Feel letting go and falling into a peaceful sleep.
- When you wake up, don't just jump up. Linger a while in your bed, experience the grogginess for a few moments. Did you dream, and if so, do you remember any of your dreams?

Tool 8: Use essential oils

There are studies that have shown that the smell of some essential oils can work as a complementary therapy to help reduce anxiety and stress. Essential oils are compounds that have been extracted from plants - the flower, herb and tree parts like bark, roots, peels, and petals. These oils capture the plant's scent and flavor, which is also referred to as its "essence". Use oils that have been obtained through distillation (via steam and/or water) or mechanical methods, such as cold pressing. Oils obtained from chemical processes are not true essential oils.

Essential oils are either inhaled, rubbed on the skin or added to a bath. When you rub it onto your skin, some of the plant chemicals are absorbed into the skin. Use a carrier oil like sweet almond oil. You can also inhale the aroma of the essential oils to stimulate areas of your limbic system (which plays a role in emotions, behaviors, sense of smell and long-term memory, as well as possibly breathing, heart rate and blood pressure). You can also add a few drops of essential oil to your bath water, in an air diffuser or light an aromatherapy candle. Reed diffusers are great to fill your home or office with scent.

While there are more than 90 different essential oils, each with its own unique smell and potential benefits, there are a few that will aid in relaxation and stress management:

- **Lavender** (Lavendula angustifolia) is used for stress relief and improving sleep.
- **Bergamot** (Citrus bergamia) is used for stress relief and improving skin conditions (like eczema). It can also help with insomnia and reducing agitation.
- **Rose** (Rosa damascena) is used to improve your mood and reduce anxiety. It also helps with panic attacks, grieving and shock.
- **Chamomile** (Chamaemelum nobile) is used for improving mood and relaxation. It can also help to decrease irritability, overthinking, anxiety and worry.
- **Ylang Ylang** (Cananga odorata) is calming and uplifting. Note of caution: it can be irritating to the skin and do not use it in conditions of low blood pressure.

SIDE NOTE: ESSENTIAL OILS DISCLAIMER

Essential oils are natural products and are not intended to diagnose, treat, cure, or prevent any disease, including autoimmune diseases. It is a complementary therapy for managing symptoms, not a treatment. Remember that essential oils are powerful compounds that some people or animals may have reactions to. Never use essential oils undiluted or ingest them without the guidance of a professional. Always read up on the side effects of the essential oils you want to use before actually using them. Don't use essential oils during the first trimester of pregnancy, or on small babies, or on people who have allergies to the plants the oils are derived from. If you see any reaction, stop using the essential oil products immediately and contact your doctor.

Tool 9: Infrared sauna therapy

You may be familiar with the idea of a sauna – it's a room filled with steam and heated to warm up your body and make you sweat. It is great way to help you detox, promote relaxation and to refresh yourself.

There are two types of saunas – the traditional sauna and an infrared sauna. An infrared sauna works differently from a normal sauna as it uses infrared waves to create heat, while the normal sauna uses a wood stove or electric heater to heat the air. The normal saunas heat the air up to approximately to 70-100 degrees Celsius (160-210 degrees Fahrenheit) compared to the infrared saunas that only heat up to 40-60 degrees Celsius (104-140 degrees Fahrenheit). The heat generated from the infrared sauna penetrates the skin far deeper and stimulates a much more vigorous sweat than the traditional sauna.

There are many benefits to going in an infrared sauna. When looking at stress reduction, infrared sauna therapy promotes relaxation by helping to balance the body's level of cortisol, the body's primary stress hormone. You will also relax and de-stress as the heat helps to release tension and relax your muscles. Other benefits of using an infrared sauna include pain relief, detoxification, wound healing and cell regeneration. After using an infrared sauna, you should have worked up a good sweat and feel better. If you feel worse, faint, fatigued, dizzy, weak or dehydrated, the session was probably too long, and you need to adjust your treatment duration

Children, elderly people and pregnant woman should not use an infrared sauna. There are also other times when you should not consider using a sauna: certain medications (so always check with your doctor first if you are not sure), if you are prone to bleeding, have a fever or a heart condition, if you are menstruating or have breast implants.

Tool 10: Become unbusy

Busyness has become a badge of honor. If you are not busy, you are not part of the group to show how on target you are to achieving your goals and how important you are. Busyness is the valid and acceptable excuse for the non-stop activity that we fill our days with. This hive of activity also creates a tremendous amount of stress.

But what if we stop all this busyness?

The antidote to busyness is nothingness. More specifically, practice doing nothing. If you don't know where you are going to fit it into your busy schedule, it is time to schedule a time to do nothing (are you seeing the irony of this suggestion?)

But how do you do nothing?

First, schedule time to do nothing. Then commit to it. If you are an extremist in busyness, you will need to schedule the time in your diary to be unbusy. It doesn't matter how long it is, but what matters is that you put it in your diary, and that you stick to it. Second, don't pick up your phone. That's it. You will be amazed about how many times you can do nothing when you don't pick up your phone.

Here are a few suggestions on what you can do when you want to do nothing. The best thing is, it is all free, which really does prove that the best things in life are free. The following ideas have been inspired by the book, *The Book of Idle Pleasures* by Dan Kieran and Tom Hodgkinson:

- Watch other people. Sit on a bench in a park or in a coffee shop where you can watch the world go by. Observe the mothers and babies, the busy professionals in their suits and computers, and the old couple who are still holding hands after 50 years of marriage.
- Take a bath. A long and relaxing bath where you soak your body in warm water. Add a handful of Epsom salts. Light a candle or two if you like, sprinkle rose petals in the water and linger. Remember to stare at the ceiling.

- Sit in the late afternoon sun in a deckchair or a hammock. While the sun is making you feel warm and relaxed, allow the stresses and thoughts of your to-do list to float away with the clouds.
- Lie on the grass and watch the clouds. As you watch the clouds, reconnect to your inner child and see the animals and shapes in the clouds. As the clouds move about their path, the shapes make a fluid transition to other shapes.
- Walk barefoot on grass. Take off your shoes, stretch out your toes and take a stroll on the grass. Feel the life force under your feet as you wander about, and how the grass tickles your toes.
- Think of what is, what could be, what if and what you would like to do. No filters, just ideas, and dreams. Who knows what inspiration and creativity will strike while you are allowing your mind to wander.
- Visit an old church. There is something very special about spending time in an old church and appreciating the beautifully carved wood, architecture and stained glass. Then sit and stare and daydream for as long as you want. You don't even have to be religious to do this.
- Fold paper planes and throw them. Take a blank sheet of paper and craft a paper plane by folding it and folding it again. If others are with you, encourage them to fold their own and have a competition to see whose plane travels the longest distance.
- Watch the birds. The doves in the city Centre, the seagulls at the harbor, or the birds in your garden. Watch as they flutter about, look for food or call for their mates.

- Stargazing. Doing nothing is not just limited to the daytime. At night, go outside, lie on a blanket on the grass or sit on your deckchair and gaze at the stars. Take a moment to appreciate the universe, getting lost in the vastness of stars and planets. You don't even have to know the names of the stars and planets!
- Read gravestones. Visit a cemetery and walk through the graveyard. Observe the names and dates of people who once were and imagine the lives that they may have lived and left behind.

Action Steps

1. Get a daily dose of sunshine.

Be in direct sunshine for 10 to 20 minutes a day. Sunshine helps with forming vitamin D, and it feels good too! If you live in a country where there is no sunshine in winter, consider blue light therapy as a replacement.

2. Free up time by clearing your diary.

Busyness is not a badge of honor. Stress and too many things to do often go together, so I want to encourage you to take some time to clear out your diary and your to-do list. You can only recover if you have time to rest. Be critical about everything you do, and act:

- What can you remove?
- What can you reduce?
- What can you outsource?
- What can you automate?
- What can you delegate?

3. Plan your week.

This is not about starting to fill up your diary again. No, this is about being selfish and planning to do things so that it works for you, balancing out the things that you have to do and want to do, that give you time for balance and rest. It is about taking control of your time and your life, so that you are exposed to less.

4. **Take a daily walk or exercise, depending how much energy you have.**

If you're low on energy, take a 10 min walk outside in the sun. If you have a little more energy, do something you enjoy, but don't overdo it. Try to do this every day, but if you miss a day for whatever reason, don't stress! Just do it, as and when you can! As you feel your energy returning, increase the speed of your walk or start to do the other activities that you like to do. Again, don't overdo it, just enough to make you feel good, happy and energized! As you start to exercise more, also make sure you take glutathione or NAC, vitamin A, C and E through a varied diet or with supplements.

5. **Get a daily dose of happiness.**

Do one thing today that makes you happy. It can be spending some time with a friend, playing with your pet, going for a hike in a park or trail, start reading a little from a book you have been wanting to read or learning something new. If you have a hobby such as photography, painting, gardening, cooking new recipes, whatever it is, start taking this up!

6. **Stop worrying about things or events that are out of your control.**

Focus on what is in your control, which are your actions and your reactions to things that happen to you.

7. Self-care Sunday

Self-care Sunday doesn't have to be on a Sunday. Pick a day of the week or in the month and schedule that day to be the day that you focus on yourself. On this day, you must detach from work, focus on the important things that bring you to you and that feed your soul.

8. Decide that good enough is good enough.

Let go of the idea of being perfect! It is exhausting. Adopt a good-enough attitude and start enjoying life!

9. Infrared or hot sauna therapy for detoxing and destressing.

A sauna (hot or infrared) is a great way to sweat, helping the body to remove toxins. Start with 5-minute sessions and build up to 20-minute sessions and remember to hydrate. Check with your doctor before you start using a sauna.

10. Find moments of being mindful.

By focusing on the present, you can calm your body and mind! Short meditations (even just a few minutes of focusing on deep breathing), mindful eating and mindful sleeping are all strategies you can adopt to be more mindful and present.

11. Use essential oils to reduce the impact of anxiety and stress

Essential oils are a wonderful complementary therapy to reduce stress and anxiety. You can burn an aromatherapy candle, add oils to an air diffuser, use a reed diffuser or add a few drops to your bath water. Try lavender, bergamot, rose, chamomile and Ylang Ylang.

12. Become unbusy.

Create time to do nothing. The antidote to busyness is nothingness. Some of my favorite things to do when I need to do nothing is watching people, taking a bath, relaxing while watching the sun set, visiting an old church, taking a walk in nature and stargazing. Experiment and find what works for you!

CHAPTER 12: PILLAR 7 - TOXINS

It's not the fish, it's the water!

Imagine a beautiful healthy goldfish in a bowl of clean water. The fish is healthy and happy. But what will happen if we never clean the water? Slowly, the water becomes polluted. What will happen if we leave the fish in the polluted water and the water is never cleaned? Would the fish be able to stay healthy? Would you agree with me that the fish will slowly become ill? Perhaps even die?

What will you do to get the fish back to health? Would you treat the fish or clean the water?

If you are like me, you would focus first on cleaning the water! After all, what would it help to treat the fish with medication without cleaning the water? So, clean the water!

We need to adopt the same approach to our health. We need to "clean our water". We have many systems that pollute our "water", including air pollution, the poor-quality food we eat and all the things we use in our homes, and even our personal care products!

We need to "clean the water".

Our bodies are always adapting to the environment, and when the body becomes stressed and not in a safe space, it is going to slow you down. For example, when the body senses that there is a famine and that food is scarce (which can also happen if you are not eating enough), the body goes into survival mode. It slows down your metabolism in order to preserve energy. You start to feel lethargic and tired, as it is not beneficial to have energy and run around doing things when there is no food available to replenish the spent energy!

In addition, there are also toxins in the environment. Another word for toxins is chemicals. While you may have a genetic predisposition for Hashi's, and while your diet also plays a part, it is the chemicals in our environment that have a huge impact on our health and our body's ability to stay healthy. Some of these chemicals directly impact the functioning of the thyroid gland. Chemicals can mimic hormones and disrupt your endocrine system, impact the gut and even affect the immune system.

There are over 77,000 chemicals used in thousands of products, and we cannot possibly review each chemical and its impact on the body. What we can do is look at a few of the chemicals that have the biggest impact on our bodies and our health.

Your body is detoxing all the time

Your body is amazing, and it does a great job of preventing and removing toxins. Your skin provides a barrier to harmful substances, your airways trap and expel noxious particles, your intestines remove harmful organisms, the liver filters out toxins in the blood and the kidneys help to filter out toxins via urine. But with toxins coming into the body from just about every angle, and certain chemicals putting even more strain on the body, your body can become overloaded with contaminants. It can only do so much to clear toxins and can struggle to do so effectively.

Luckily, we can do much to help our body's natural ability to remove toxins. Detox pathways are the different ways or routes that your body uses to get rid of toxins, which include breath, urine, sweat and bowel movements. You need to make sure that these pathways are working well and are not backed up or clogged.

The role of the liver

There is one organ in our bodies that works super hard to clear out toxins, and that organ is the liver. We can help the liver to do its job by lessening the toxic load and keeping it healthy.

When you expose yourself to toxins every day and sometimes even multiple times a day (like using antibacterial hand-wash multiple times a day), the risk is that the toxins become too much for the liver to remove effectively. The liver becomes congested! Toxins start to build up in the liver, and you may start to experience symptoms like digestive problems, bad breath, excessive sweating, weight gain or weight loss, dizziness, hair loss, heartburn, and skin breakouts to name just a few. You may also experience right-sided chest pain, gas and diarrhea.

Remember that the liver also plays an important role in converting inactive T4 thyroid hormone to the active T3 thyroid hormone. If your liver is not working like it is supposed to, the conversion of T4 to T3 hormones will be impacted.

You may be tempted or may have been advised to do a liver cleanse or detox, like chelation protocol, coffee enemas, fasting or high doses of iodine. If you are not feeling well, these hard and forceful measures may make you feel worse. It can release too many toxins from where they are stored too quickly and overwhelm your liver, making you feel worse.

Taking care of your liver

You may have also heard about fatty liver, and more specifically non-alcoholic fatty liver disease (acronym NAFLD). Fatty liver was originally thought to be an alcoholics disease, but fatty liver can also occur from other causes. Research suggests a strong link between hypothyroidism and fatty liver disease, as proper thyroid function is vital for fat metabolism, and proper liver function is needed for thyroid hormone conversion.

I want to stress this: non-alcoholic fatty liver disease is not caused by dietary fat. The cause has been found to be too many carbs and too many sugars, especially the sugar found in junk food and soft drinks. High cholesterol and diabetes have also been linked to NAFLD. The bad news is that people with underactive thyroid (hypothyroidism) are at risk of non-alcoholic fatty liver disease, because of the effect of the underactive thyroid on fat metabolism and liver function.

There are several things that you can do to help support your liver:

1. Avoid foods that can put strain on your liver, including gluten, dairy, sugar, soy, alcohol and coffee. You will lower the inflammation in your body and help the liver in its role to remove toxins.
2. Eat foods that provide nutrients to help your liver, including hot lemon water, beets, cilantro, green juices, fermented foods, cruciferous vegetables, turmeric and berries.
3. Check for toxins in your home and at work and avoid and remove as many toxins as you possibly can.
4. Avoid strong detox programs, such as high dose iodine, coffee enemas or chelating agents like spirulina. High doses of iodine can increase thyroid gland destruction, while coffee enemas can result in perforated bowels or colitis and inflammation of the gut lining.

Take care of your liver. It does an extremely important job in removing toxins from your body, and it also plays a role in converting the inactive T4 hormone to the active T3 hormone. You want your liver to work well!

The toxins in our bodies

Mercury

Dental amalgam fillings (also known as silver fillings) are one of the main sources of mercury in our bodies that has a detrimental impact on the thyroid gland. Amalgam on average contains 50% mercury by weight, and then also silver (about 30%) and the remainder is other elements like copper. What is the impact of mercury? Let's start with every time you eat. Trace elements of mercury go through the gum and are swallowed. The body absorbs the mercury and it goes through the intestinal wall into the body, impacting the thyroid, the adrenal glands and the pituitary gland. The thyroid gland absorbs mercury and as it is similar in structure to iodine, it can trigger an immune system reaction and slow the function of the thyroid gland.

The question is, if you have amalgam fillings, should you consider getting them it removed? Yes. Absolutely. There is no doubt that you must get them removed. I recommend you consult a biological dentist to remove the fillings. A biological dentist will take the necessary precautions when removing the fillings, like providing an oxygen mask, skin cover, extra suction and targeted supplements to bind the mercury residue. If the removal process is not done correctly, you can breathe in mercury vapor. You will get a big dose of mercury in your body, which can trigger a Hashi's flare up. Other sources of mercury include contaminated tuna, rice and some corn by-products (like high-fructose corn syrup), cosmetics, vaccines, and coal-powered power stations that add to environmental pollution.

Breast Implants

If you have had breast implant surgery and have experienced Hashi's symptoms afterwards, it could be that the implants are a trigger. Breast implants are typically made from silicone gel or saline, but also include other chemicals. According to Breast Implant Illness, there are more than 40 toxic chemicals and heavy metals used in the manufacturing process of breast implants. Unfortunately, research has found that both saline and silicone breast implants can bleed heavy metals leading to wide-spread inflammation in the body. If you are worried that your breast implants may be the cause of your Hashi's, speak with your functional doctor. You may need to consider having the implants removed to get your health back.

Other heavy metals

Our bodies can build up heavy metals. The liver may not be able to clear them out fast enough, and they stay in the body and can become toxic. Which metals are we talking out? In addition to mercury, there are three chemicals that have no known beneficial effect in humans: arsenic, cadmium and lead. As with mercury, these chemicals are confirmed as probable carcinogens, and these chemicals have a wide-ranging toxic impact on the body, negatively affecting your immune, endocrine, nervous, renal, musculoskeletal and cardiovascular systems. Your doctor should be able to do a test to see if your body is affected and if you have a toxic burden.

The toxins from our food

Pesticides and herbicides

Pesticides are chemicals used to kill bacteria, insects, plant diseases and fungi, to name a few. Herbicides are chemicals used to kill weeds or undesirable plants. Some herbicides are designed to kill anything they touch, while others are designed to kill specific plants. Many of the foods we eat have pesticides and herbicides sprayed on them without us being aware. For example:

- Pesticides are sprayed onto crops to keep them free from insects, bacteria and plant diseases in order to increase the harvest. Unless you are making sure you buy organic food or you have washed your food well before cooking with it or eating it, you are at risk of ingesting these toxic pesticides.
- Herbicides are used to kill unwanted plants. Glyphosate (the common brand name is Roundup) is the most used herbicide on crops, and it is a toxin. In order to protect the crops, seeds are genetically modified to be resistant to glyphosate. This means that producers can comfortably spray their crops with glyphosate without the worry that they may lose their crops.

In addition to seeds being genetically modified to be resistant to glyphosate, the food itself has been engineered to be a pesticide! This means that when a bug eats this plant, it will die because the pesticide is in each and every cell of the plant. And then we eat these foods. This is scary, right?

Luckily not all fruits and vegetables are exposed to pesticides and herbicides or have been genetically modified. Have you heard of the Dirty Dozen™ and the Clean Fifteen™? These are lists of fruits and vegetables published annually by the Environmental Working Group (EWG), an American non-profit organization dedicated to protecting human health as well as the environment. The Dirty Dozen™ gives you the top 12 foods that have the highest exposure to herbs and pesticides, and the Clean Fifteen™ list details the foods which have the lowest levels of exposure.

The best option is to eat organic (pesticide and herbicide free) fruits and vegetables. If you cannot afford to buy organic produce, then consider buying it for your children to limit their toxic exposure. Children are more susceptible to neurotoxins as their brains are still developing. What is frightening is that pesticide exposure places children at a higher risk to a variety of chronic conditions, as well as behavior and learning issues.

Some produce can contain more than 50 types of pesticides. If you cannot buy organic produce at all, consider loading up first on the produce that is on the Clean Fifteen™ list which has the lowest levels of pesticides. But should you stop eating the food that is on the Dirty Dozen™ list? No! Eating a variety of vegetables is very important for your health, and many experts in the nutrition field still believe that the benefits of eating a variety of vegetables still outweighs the risk of pesticide exposure. The trick is to ensure that you adequately clean the produce that is on the Dirty Dozen list before cooking with it or eating it.

You can clean your produce at home using a natural fruit and vegetable wash that is available at most health stores, or make your own using vinegar and water or bicarbonate of soda and water.

Becoming toxic from too much healthy food

Did I get your attention with this heading? Yes, the principle of "too much of a good thing" really applies here. Can you get sick from food? Yes, you absolutely can. One such food is kale. Yes, the mighty and healthy kale.

Many people believe that kale is so good for you that you should have it with every meal. The problem with kale is that it is high in sulphur. Sulphur is good for you as it aids in the detoxification processes of the body. But if you eat it as part of a healthy diet with other high-sulphur foods such as meat, eggs and certain greens, you may have a sulphur overload.

Which other foods contain have a high sulphur content? Leafy greens, including spinach, and cruciferous vegetables like broccoli. Then there are proteins like egg and shrimp. Other foods that have a high sulphur content are beer, wine and pickled foods.

How do you know if you have a sulphur overload? As the body is trying to get rid of the sulphur, you may experience a histamine reaction, which can manifest as itchy skin, hives, swelling or eczema. Early signs include headaches, itchy skin (without the rash), digestive issues and even feelings of anxiety. A diet like the Paleo diet may cause sulphites to build up in the body over time, and then suddenly a person may have a reaction which seems unexplainable! And remember that we are all different, so not everyone who eats kale and spinach regularly will experience a sulphur overload.

How can you help your body to detox from the sulphur? There are two recommendations by Inna Topiler. First, take a warm bath with a cup and a half of Epsom salts and soak for 20 minutes, and do this every day or every other day. Second, you can use charcoal tablets to help absorb the ammonia caused by the sulphur. You can also take a molybdenum supplement to help support the enzymes that process the sulphites. Lastly, bring in more variety of leafy greens to balance out the kale.

The toxins around us

There are many things in and around our environment (work and home) that add to the toxic load in our bodies. When we are exposed to a toxin, our body does an exceptional job to clear it, and our liver plays a key role in this process. But when we are exposed to toxins every day, and sometimes multiple times per day, the body still works to clear it, but the exposure may become too much. Then the toxins build up in the body. It's like a runaway train – regardless of how hard the body is working to clear them out, it just seems like a never-ending stream of toxins flooding the body.

Let's have a look at some of the most common toxins that may be in your immediate environment: your home, at your place of work, the products you use in your personal care and even your cooking utensils.

Mold

Mold can show up in many places. Firstly, in the food that we consume, for example coffee and oats. Secondly, in our homes, where areas of moisture are not well-ventilated. How do you know if you have mold in your home? Firstly, you can smell it - a stale, moldy smell in the house or the room. Secondly, you can see it - visible mold growth in areas like showers. Mold blackens the grout lines in the shower, it discolors dry walling, it can show up as black spots on siding, it darkens wooden decks and it rots damp wood. It often starts as mildew, which is tiny, usually black spots. You can quickly check if it is mildew by dabbing a few drops of household bleach on the blackened area. If it lightens after one or two minutes, it is mold.

If you suspect the mold may be adding to the toxic load in your body, you will need to look at what you can do to remove it. Check your living space and your place of work. When you suspect there is mold, address it immediately. Some mold you can remove yourself, but if it is at your place of work or too severe, have a professional service remove it.

If you live in a rented place and you have tried everything you can to remove the mold, speak to the owner to address it. If the owner is not willing to deal with it, this is the point where I recommend that you start looking for another place to stay as quickly as possible. It is just not worth the risk to live in a home or work in a place where there is mold.

Personal care products and cosmetics

We put creams on our skins, wash our bodies with soaps and brush our teeth with toothpaste. All these personal care products like nail polish, body wash, soap, lotion, make up, makeup remover, shampoo, conditioner, toothpaste, perfume, nail polish remover, and shaving cream to name a few, are all loaded with chemicals. Do you know if any of the personal care products you use could be making you sick? Such as the shampoo that gives your hair that beautiful shine? The SPF 50 sunscreen you use? That lovely nice-smelling body lotion you apply? Most of these products are loaded with toxic chemicals. Even some baby shampoo is full of toxic chemicals!

Skincare products can be a big source of toxicity. There are approximately 168 different chemicals used in skincare products. The creams and lotions we put on are absorbed into the body without passing through the liver first. Whatever you put on to your skin, ends up in your body. Many of the big companies state that the doses of the toxic chemicals are small enough that they won't impact your health. The problem is that you are not just using a single product. You are using many products, many times a day. Also, many of the chemicals in personal care products have not undergone safety studies to prove that they are non-toxic. Not all chemicals are dangerous, but there are chemicals that are carcinogens (can cause cancer), neurotoxins and reproductive toxins (proven to interfere with brain development and reproduction in animals).

Here are a few of the biggest chemical villains that you should try to avoid:

- *Triclosan*: This is a common chemical that is used in the manufacture of antibacterial soaps, deodorants, toothpastes and even hair sprays. It is similar to the structure of thyroid hormones and can cause disruption with the hormones in your body. The USA has banned triclosan due to thyroid toxicity.

- *Heavy meals and metalloids*: Heavy metals like lead, cadmium and mercury to name a few, are toxic to the body. These are found in personal care products as well as supplements.
- *Xenoestrogens*: These are chemicals that mimic the effect of estrogen in your body. It is not only found in skincare products, but in a multitude of other products, like soy, PBA, and plastics. It causes havoc with your hormones!
- *Fluoride*: Fluoride is found in most toothpastes and many governments have put fluoride in the water. You can also find fluoride in some medications, and even in black, green and red tea. The problem is that fluoride suppresses thyroid function.

European governments required the removal of many toxic chemicals from products. Some of these chemicals include hydroabietyl alcohol, dibutyl phthalate, verbena oil, petroleum distillates and catalase. But in other countries there are still many products that may include these chemicals. We have to become familiar with some of the names of these chemicals, and vote with our money. Don't buy these products.

There are some sites and apps available that can help us to understand whether a product has harmful chemicals in it, and how much of it is contained in the product. Once such website is https://www.ewg.org/skindeep/search where you can search for your product and see how it is rated.

Let's move on to cosmetics. I love my makeup, and it was frightening to find out how many chemicals are in the products that I love! And these are big brand companies who have significant money for research and development. You would think that they would invest money into researching and developing clean products! But alas, currently that doesn't seem to be happening. Luckily there are new brands who are fighting the good fight and who are providing a safer alternative. One site that I appreciate is http://www.safecosmetics.org/. Here you will find the Red List – the top toxic chemicals in the different product categories, including shampoo, conditioner, creams, sunscreen, color cosmetics, hair color and skin lighters.

So, what can you do? The solution is simple. Ditch the products with the toxic chemicals and buy products that have lower levels of chemicals or that have been verified as clean. Your health (and your liver and your thyroid gland) will thank you for it!

Plastic products

Plastic is the one thing that most people make use of everyday. You can find it in just about every kitchen. It is cheap, useful, doesn't break like glass and is easy to clean. You will find plastic products in cooking utensils, food containers and even containers used in preparing or reheating food in the microwave oven. But not all plastic products are the same.

Plastic products have an identification triangle with a number in it, so you can identify the type of plastic used. This number is not about the level of toxicity – it refers to the type of plastic used. Let's have a look at each of these labels in more detail, and which plastic we can use and which ones we should avoid.

- *BPA (Bisphenol A, falls under the category #7 Other Plastic)*: BPA is a well-known plastic that is found in containers, baby formula cans and even in the coating of paper receipts. It is also known as polycarbonates. BPA has been found to be an endocrine disrupter and it has been linked to cancers, reproductive disorders as well as developmental disorders. When this plastic is heated, it can leach toxins up to 55 times the rate compared to when it is not heated. Also, watch out for scratched and old plastic that contain BPA, as it will leach toxins. Many manufacturers have now developed BPA-free products, which we thought were better. But are they really better?
- *Bisphenol S (BPS) and bisphenol B (BPB), both falls under the category #7 Other Plastic*: When BPA was prohibited in the manufacturing and sale of plastic products, manufacturers started using bisphenol S (BPS) and bisphenol B (BPB) as alternatives. I have seen many plastic products labelled as "BPA Free" and thought it was a better product to use. Research found that BPB and BPS were also toxic, and specifically neurotoxic. So, even if the label states it is PBA-Free, check to see if it is made from BPS or BPB. If it is, best you don't buy it.
- *Polyvinyl chloride plastics (PVC, #3 plastic)* commonly contain a toxin called phthalates, which is added to make plastic more flexible. You know the plastic food wrap that you use to cover your food? Yes, that is PVC. Unfortunately, the phthalates in plastic wraps get into your fatty foods such as meat and cheese. Other plastic products that contain phthalates include soft toys for babies (often used as it is soft on the baby's mouth), products

made with vinyl (thinking waterproof clothing) and squeeze toys. The harder PVC products, such as vinyl flooring and harder PVC toys, contains another group of toxic chemicals called organotin compounds. These chemicals are used as a stabilizer in PVC, agricultural fungicides, wood preservatives, paints and even rodent repellents. PVC products are not recyclable either. From a health perspective, it is not called the "poison plastic" for no reason, as it contains numerous toxins that are immunotoxic and cause hormonal changes.

- *Polystyrene (#6 plastic)* is another toxic plastic. Polystyrene is used in packaging containers, think about when you get take-away food. There are two types of polystyrene: extruded polystyrene (commonly known as Styrofoam) and the non-extruded polystyrene (which is a clear disposable plastic). The toxins in polystyrene are styrene and benzene, which are considered possible carcinogens and are also hormone disrupters. Never heat polystyrene in a microwave oven. Actually, just avoid it completely.
- *Single use plastics* are typically Polyethylene terephthalate (PET or PETE, #1 plastic) or HD Polyethylene (HDPE, #2 plastic). Examples of single use plastics include straws, plastic lids, plastic grocery bags, plastic beverage bottles and plastic bottle caps. The idea is that these plastics are used once and then thrown away and recycled. While recycling is done, these plastics end up in the oceans and landfills as the recycling isn't done fast enough. These plastics also leach chemicals when exposed to UV and as it naturally breaks down over time. HDPE does not break down in

sunlight or with extreme heat or freezing. Never reuse these plastics, put them in the sun or put hot food or beverages in them.

- *Low-density Polyethylene (LDPE, #4 plastic)* is considered safe, but it is not environmentally friendly as it is made from toxic industrial chemicals, including butane, benzene and vinyl acetate. This plastic is found in dry cleaning garment bags, squeezable bottles and the plastic bags used to package bread. While this plastic is reusable, it is not always recyclable.
- *Polypropylene (PP, #5 plastic)* is the safest plastic as it is heat resistant. It is unlikely to leach even when it is exposed to warm or hot water. While it is safe to use for food, this plastic is not accepted by most recycling centers.

The best option is to avoid plastic products. In your kitchen, replace the plastic food storage containers with glass and ceramic cookware. Replace the plastic wrap with reusable beeswax strips, and replace your plastic cooking utensils with bamboo, wood or platinum food-grade silicone utensils. And for your daily coffee or tea take-away, avoid using the once-off plastic cups and lids and get your own reusable take-away cup, ideally with a silicone lid.

Cooking utensils and cookware

I used to love my Teflon-coated cookware. It is easy to use and easy to clean. But every time you cook with a Teflon-coated pan, toxins are released into the food. There are alternatives to Teflon-coated pans. You can use stainless steel, enamel-coated cookware, cast iron, carbonated steel, clay and glass cookware. Stainless steel is a better alternative than Teflon-coated cookware but be careful as nickel from the stainless-steel pans may be a problem for some.

Cooking utensils can also be a source of toxins. Plastic utensils can melt from heat and leach toxins into your food. Change your cooking utensils to those made from wood, bamboo, stainless steel and food-grade silicone products.

Cleaning products and air fresheners

Conventional cleaning products are full of toxic chemicals. Halogens and halogen-containing chemicals can impact the function of the thyroid gland as these chemicals are similar in structure to iodine. It can lead to inflammation of the thyroid gland and even thyroid cell death.

The three main chemicals in cleaning products that we need to avoid are chlorine, bromide and fluoride. Chlorine is used in many products, including pool chemicals, cleaning products and plastics. It increases TSH hormones, thyroid antibodies and can impact the size of the thyroid.

While synthetic air fresheners make your home smell wonderful, it is not thyroid-friendly. Most artificial fragrances are a cocktail full of chemicals that you breathe in. You can make your own cleaning solutions, or purchase cleaning products that are made from natural ingredients.

Flame retardant products

Bromide, also known as the flame-retardant chemical, is another halogen-containing chemical that impacts the functioning of the thyroid gland. You can find bromide in mattresses and fabrics that are flame-retardant, and even in baked goods and soft drinks!

Aluminum

Aluminum is another toxin you need to be aware of since many people use aluminum foil when cooking in the oven. Aluminum can also be found in cooking pans, as well as anti-perspirants, and some antacids may also contain aluminum.

Air pollution

Air pollution is not just about factory gasses and the gas from car exhaust pipes. The quality of the air you breathe at home and at work can also be toxic to your health. Do you like that new carpet and new car smell? Not good. These smells are toxic gasses that are released from the materials they were made from.

Other things that can cause air pollution are faulty air-conditioning and ventilation systems, pollen and VOCs (volatile organic compounds) from paints, thinners, cigarettes, cleaning products, air fresheners, adhesives, wood preservatives, glues and pesticides. VOCs are also released by burning fuels such as petrol, diesel, wood and goal.

VOCs are not good for your health. But how do you know if you are exposed to VOCs? Some of the symptoms you may experience include headaches, dizziness, memory problems, visual disorders and irritation of the eyes and respiratory tract. Over the long term, exposure to VOCs can lead to nausea, fatigue, loss of coordination, damage to the liver, kidneys and central nervous system, and even cancer.

Radiation

We are exposed to radiation from various sources. Radiation is part of the earth and there are radioactive gases in the air we breathe. Even in our bodies there are naturally occurring radioactive elements. But the radiation that we need to be cognizant of is man-made radiation, such as X-rays and radiation that is used to diagnose diseases and treat cancer. Then there are also radioactive materials that can cause serious harm to us, like uranium and radium.

Radiation can damage the body depending on the type of radiation. While we cannot eliminate the natural radiation that occurs, we can protect ourselves from the impact of deliberate radiation, like wearing protective gear when you need to go for X-rays, and a throat protector when you visit your dentist and X-rays are taken of your teeth.

New clothes

Have you ever bought clothes and smelled them? Chemicals, and sometimes, a lot of them! David Andrews, a senior scientist with the non-profit Environmental Working Group, investigated the use of chemicals in the textile industry. He found that clothing is often treated with stain-repellents, color-fasteners, anti-wrinkle agents, softness-enhancers, and any number of other chemical treatments. Many of these chemicals are irritants to the skin and can have other impacts on your health as well.

Should you do a detox?

So, let's discuss detoxing. When I researched the topic of detoxification, I was overwhelmed with ideas and terms like methylation, coffee enemas, autophagy, chelation therapy, activated charcoal, glutathione, juice cleanses, intermitted fasting, cryotherapy, ketosis, chemical tolerance, castor oil and milk thistle! This is insane, right? So how do we make sense of what to do when we want to give our bodies the best support in detoxifying?

First, let's understand what we mean with detoxification, as it can be just as confusing as the word "diet". Firstly, we need to remember that our bodies detoxify all day, every day, to neutralize, transform and remove toxins. The liver plays a key role in removing the toxins from the body, and sometimes the toxic load can be too much for the liver to handle effectively, and the toxins remain in the body. The toxins come from everywhere – our homes, our food, our workplaces, even in the air we breathe! So, while the body generally does well to remove these toxins, with the constant onslaught of contaminants, we may need to give the body a boost, to help remove these poisons from the body.

Before we investigate how we help our bodies to detox, there are also different phases of detoxification that the body goes through:

- **Phase 1, oxidation**, is your first line of defense against toxins: a group of enzymes known as the cytochrome P450 family. These enzymes protect your cells from damage by breaking down harmful toxins into less harmful and smaller forms so that the toxins are water soluble for excretion in phase 2. The toxins become free radicals, which if not quickly addressed in phase 2, can cause a lot of damage in your body.
- **Phase 2 is called conjugation**, and it is all about taking the products from phase 1 and binding them into less harmful substances so that the body can eliminate them. These substances include amino acids, sugars, glutathione, methionine, sulphur and acetyl co-A.
- **Phase 3 is about transporting** the phase 2 conjugates out of the body, either through urine or your stool. A healthy gut is imperative for this phase to work effectively.

If any of these phases is not working optimally and effectively, your body will not be able to remove toxins, they will build up and you will not feel well and may even become very ill. Symptoms may include an autoimmune flare-up, fatigue, insomnia, anxiety, dizziness, migraines and constipation.

We therefore need to make sure that the three phases of the detoxification process work. But the way to make sure your body can process all these toxins is counter-intuitive: we first need to make sure that phase 3 works well! It does not help to focus on phase 1 and 2 when your body is not able to remove this toxic waste from your body in the first place!

Here is what you can do to help the different phases:

- Starting with phase 3, enjoy cruciferous vegetables, oranges, apples and grapefruit – they all have calcium-D-glucarate and glutaric acid. Milk thistle contains silymarin, which also helps in this phase.
- Focusing on phase 2, include foods in your diet that have natural sulphur such as eggs and cruciferous vegetables like broccoli and cauliflower. Raw garlic, onions, leeks and shallots are also useful sources. Flavonoids found in fruits, vegetables and many herbs are also helpful. But sometimes not even a healthy diet can provide all these benefits, and you may need to supplement with glutamine, choline and inositol.
- To support phase 1, make sure you take high quality protein, B vitamins, magnesium, selenium and zinc. As this process results in free radicals, you also need antioxidants like vitamin C, E and various carotenoids. Be careful of antacids, antihistamines, and even NSAIDS (nonsteroidal anti-inflammatory drugs) like aspirin and ibuprofen, as these medications slow down the enzymes.

So, how do you know if your toxin excretion process is working effectively? Simple – just count the number of times you are going the bathroom to 'poop'! You want it to be between every other day up to three times a day. But it not just how frequent it is that is important, it is also about what it looks like, and the Bristol stool chart (also known as the Meyers Scale) can help you, especially if you are having a conversation with your doctor about it!

Bristol Stool Chart	Description	Indicates
Type 1	Separate hard lumps, like nuts (hard to pass)	Typically means you are constipated
Type 2	Sausage-shaped, but lumpy	Another sign of constipation
Type 3	Sausage-shaped, but with cracks on the surface	Gold standard, especially if it is soft and easy to pass.
Type 4	Sausage- or snake-like, smooth and soft	Normal
Type 5	Soft blobs with clear-cut edges (easy to pass)	Lacking fiber
Type 6	Fluffy pieces with ragged edges, mushy	Could be a sign of mild diarrhea, try drinking more water
Type 7	Watery, no solid pieces (entirely liquid)	Diarrhea

The ideal type is number 3 or 4. And the color of your poop can also indicate if your body is working as it should! Any shade of brown is good, but if you are seeing other colors of the rainbow, you may want to check what is causing this.

- A little green is fine.

- A lot of green could result from adding a lot of greens to your diet, like spinach. If not, it could be that your stools are passing through too fast.
- Black is okay if you had liquorice (the herb, not the sweet), iron supplements or bismuth medications. If not, speak to your doctor as it could be a sign of bleeding in the upper gastrointestinal tract.
- Pale, white or clay-colored stool could indicate that you are lacking bile from your liver and gallbladder, and possibly a duct is blocked. Certain medications, like anti-diarrhea medication, can also make the stool look pale.
- Stools can be red if you have eaten beets, cranberries, tomato juice and even red gelatin. It can also indicate bleeding, so if it continues, consult your doctor.
- Yellow is typically a sign of too much fat, or it can indicate a malabsorption disorder like celiac disease.

I bet the next time you go to the toilet; you are going to have a look! And you should! Your poop is an immediate feedback loop to how healthy your gut is, and how well you are eating!

So should you do a focused detox?

It is not a straightforward or an easy answer. If your poop is not a number 3 or 4, then a focused detox is not for you yet. The reason is that if your body is not working effectively to get the toxins out, it can increase the free radicals in your body which can cause inflammation and tissue damage.

Also, Dr Datis Kharriazian, clinician and researcher for autoimmune disorders, believes that you must be healthy enough to do a detox. People will do a detox and then have a reaction, which they believe is a reaction from the toxins, while it may be an immune reaction. He refers to the term chemical tolerance, which is how well your body is tolerant to chemicals. People who suffer from an autoimmune disease have lost their ability to tolerate chemicals, and if those people do chelation or a heavy detox, this will make them worse.

If you want to do a detox, here are the steps:

Step 0: If you are experiencing a flare-up, don't do a detox right now. Wait until you are feeling stronger and healthier. You want the detoxing process to be gentle, and not harsh on your body. Also, remove gluten from your diet. A detox can be emotionally tough, so do it when you are prepared and ready for the challenge.

Step 1: Make sure your gut is healthy and working as it should! There is a lot of information available about your gut microbiome, so please read more about it. You can't just take an expensive probiotic supplement and think that is all you need. Here are more suggestions:

- Eat more vegetables, nuts and fresh fruits, especially oranges, apples and grapefruit.
- Brush your teeth (with fluoride-free toothpaste) and floss every day. Studies at Cornell University have found that bacteria from your mouth can cause gut problems.

- Eat fermented foods that have beneficial bacteria, like sauerkraut and kombucha.
- Eat foods with polyphenols, like red grapes, almonds, onions, blueberries, broccoli and dark chocolate (only small pieces occasionally).
- Use spices like garlic, turmeric and ginger in your cooking.
- Don't use artificial sweeteners, but you do know this already!
- Take a high-quality probiotic to help restore the balance between good and bad bacteria.
- You may need to check if you have any other food intolerances that may impact your gut function.

Step 2: Support your phase 1 and 2 detoxification processes with the right foods and supplements:

- Foods include eggs, meat, cruciferous vegetables, raw garlic, leeks and shallots. Eat a high-quality protein, like meat. Beetroot and pomegranate are foods that have a positive impact on oxidation and helping the liver to remove toxins.
- Supplement with glycine, glutamine, choline and inositol. Glutathione (an antioxidant) is also important. N-Acetyl-Cystine is the supplement that can help.
- Reduce your use of NSAIDS (nonsteroidal anti-inflammatory drugs like aspirin and ibuprofen), and limit or avoid using antacids and antihistamines. If you need to, rather use paracetamol.
- Drink a magnesium supplement, like magnesium glycinate or magnesium citrate.

- Make sure you have foods with vitamin B, C and E, selenium and zinc. You can also consider taking supplements to support the detoxification processes.

Step 3: Use the body's natural detox pathways to remove toxins, including exercise, sauna and taking regular warm baths with Epsom salts.

Step 4: Take activated charcoal to help bind toxins, especially when you exercise or use a sauna.

Wait at least an hour after taking other supplements before you take activated charcoal, as it will bind the good stuff with the bad stuff. Start with a small amount like 20 grams and take it throughout the day. If you take too much too quickly, you can experience severe constipation or laxative effects. It can also interfere with certain prescription medications, including naltrexone. If you are taking prescription medication, please check with your doctor before you take activated charcoal.

Step 5: Consider juicing or intermittent fasting for further detoxification. I am a huge supporter of juicing to support your health goals! My aim is to have at least one freshly made-at-home cold-pressed juice a day. I have also done a 30-days juice-only cleanse as well. There are many ways in which you can incorporate juicing into your life. I love a daily green juice to increase my intake of fruits and vegetables, boosting nutrients and providing essential vitamins and minerals. Then, you can boost nutrient intake, support gut healing, help promote detoxification and increase your energy with a juice-only diet for three days, a week or even a month! A balanced and nutritious juicing plan is a great way to support your healing. I am talking here about fresh fruit juices, made at home with a slow or cold-pressed juicer and a blender.

Intermittent fasting is also an excellent way of supporting your body, but I will not recommend it if you are having a flare-up or if you are not well on your way in your healing journey. Intermittent fasting can put a lot of stress on your body, and if your thyroid antibodies are high and you are not feeling well, I will recommend you avoid intermittent fasting. It is not for everyone, so speak to your doctor, dietician or nutritionist before starting any intermittent fasting protocol.

Should you consider chelation therapy?

Chelation therapy refers to the use of chelating drugs to treat heavy metal poisoning and neurotoxicity. Interestingly, the term "chelator" originated from the Greek word "chele", which means claw.

There is controversy around chelation therapy. While chelation therapy is very effective for removing lead, mercury, aluminum, arsenic, iron and copper, it can put a huge strain on your liver and kidneys and you can get very ill from the process if your liver and kidneys cannot process the metals. It may trigger serious side effects such as kidney damage and abnormally low blood levels of calcium.

Most doctors will only consider this treatment if you have moderate to severe heavy metal poisoning. An example of when you may need to consider chelation therapy is when you have an MRI contrast done, as the contrast agent contains metals that can deposit in the brain and you will require chelation to remove these metals. If you have been exposed to a lot of heavy metals and you want to consider chelation therapy, please talk to your doctor and only do it under your doctor's guidance and supervision.

Action Steps

1. **Filter your water for drinking and cooking.**

   Normal tap water is treated with chemicals such as chlorine to kill bacteria, and many countries have added fluoride in the general water supply. Then there is the seepage of pesticides and herbicides into the ground water, polluting our water sources. These are all toxins that our livers must remove from our bodies. One of the easiest ways to help lighten the load on your liver is to clean the water before you drink it, cook with it, and if possible, clean your body with it.

   Install a water filtration system in your kitchen or one for your home. Look for a system that you can easily be installed below the sink or outside before the water goes into the pipes that lead to the kitchen tap. Reverse osmosis systems are the most popular and are very effective at cleaning the water. A home water filtration system is a great option if your budget allows for it, as your bath and shower water are also sources where the skin can absorb toxins.

   If you cannot afford to install a water filtration system at your kitchen sink or you are renting, buy filtered water (reverse osmosis filtered) in large containers for drinking and cooking.

   Take filtered water to work in a glass jug for drinking and for making your coffee or tea. Another option is a jug with a filtration system in it so you can fill up your water at the office and still filter it before you drink it.

2. **Use fluoride free toothpaste and floss every day.**

   Fluoride and Hashi's do not go together, as fluoride is a toxin that suppresses the thyroid function. Most commercial toothpaste will have added fluoride, so I recommend you visit a health shop and speak to them about fluoride-free alternatives.

3. **Stop buying water in plastic bottles.**

   Food and beverages packaged in plastic bottles are not good for you. I recommend that you filter water at home and use a stainless-steel or glass water bottle for your water.

   On a side note, while the plastic for bottled water is recyclable, the rate at which the recycling is happening is not keeping up with the demand and most plastic bottles end up in landfills, and worse, in the oceans. Stop buying plastic bottled water and drinks.

4. **Download the Clean 15™ and Dirty Dozen™ food lists from EWC website.**

   The Environmental Working Group annually lists the shopper's guide to fruits and vegetables that are high and low in pesticides and herbicides. You can find these lists at https://www.ewg.org/foodnews/ . Download these lists and keep them on hand when you go shopping. Ideally, for any fruits and vegetables on the Dirty Dozen™ list, switch to organic options if possible. You can buy fruits and vegetables that are on the Clean Fifteen™ list without worrying too much.

5. **Wash fresh fruit and vegetables before eating or cooking with them.**

   Most non-organic fruits and vegetables are treated with pesticides and herbicides, so it is important to wash fruits and vegetables before you eat or cook with them. Rinsing under water does not remove pesticides and herbicides. I recommend a commercial fruit and vegetable wash. You can also soak your produce in a vinegar bath (one part vinegar to four parts water) or use a solution of two teaspoons of bicarbonate of soda in a bowl of water.

6. **Check for mold in your home and remove it.**

   Take a walk through your home and check for signs of mold. Mold is particularly prone in damp areas, so investigate your shower, shower curtain and walls in the bathroom. If there was water damage for whatever reason, check for signs of mold. You may also smell mold - a stale, earthy smell in the house or a particular room.

   If you do find mold, even a small amount, take action to remove it before it becomes a problem. If there are large areas of mold or black mold, consider getting professional help to remove it. To remove the mold yourself, make sure you wear the necessary protective clothing, such as a long-sleeved shirt, long pants and rubber gloves, protect your eyes with goggles and your nose and mouth with a surgery mask. With surface mold you can quickly scrub away with a 1-to-8 bleach/water solution with a little detergent added. You can also buy a mildew cleaner at hardware stores, paint stores and most home centers.

Make sure there is good ventilation in any damp areas, such as bathrooms. Paint the walls and ceilings in damp areas (like bathrooms) with paint that contains mildewcide. If you are renting, speak to your landlord about removing the mold. If the landlord is not willing to help, you may need to consider finding alternative accommodation.

7. **Relax in a bath with Epsom salts once or twice a week.**

Epsom salt is a form of magnesium and by relaxing in a hot bath with an added cup of Epsom salts you can help your body detox. You can also add a few drops of your favorite essential oil to the water to help in relaxing, detoxing and sleeping, such as lavender, Ylang Ylang or lemon essential oils.

8. **Change to non-toxic lip moisturizer and lipstick.**

Lip moisturizers and lipsticks are often loaded with toxic chemicals. A quick win is to change your lip moisturizer to a non-toxic option and change your lipstick to organic, non-toxic lipsticks. If you struggle with dry lips, you can use olive oil as a moisturizer and dab it on as needed.

9. **Wash new clothes before wearing them.**

New clothes are often full of chemicals to protect them during transport and storage. Clothing is often treated with stain-repellents, color-fasteners, anti-wrinkle agents, softness-enhancers, and any number of other chemical treatments. So, before you wear any new clothing, please wash it to remove as much of these chemicals as possible.

10. **Switch to non-toxic handwash.**

    Liquid hand soap is a staple in many homes, mine included. However, most liquid hand soaps available in the shops are loaded with toxic chemicals. You can purchase non-toxic liquid hand soap from your local health shop, or you can make your own! There are many recipes available online for home-made handwash.

11. **Use non-toxic hand sanitizer where possible.**

    Our hands touch many things during the day, and to protect yourself from spreading germs and being infected, cleaning your hands regularly is important. The problem comes with using anti-bacterial products that are loaded with toxic ingredients, like triclosan! Instead of purchasing hand sanitizers with triclosan and fragrances in, look for a non-toxic hand sanitizer at your local health shop or health online retailer.

12. **Replace silver dental fillings with the help of a biological dentist.**

    Mercury dental fillings are for many a source of toxicity. If you have any silver fillings in your teeth, I recommend that you have them removed and replaced with safer alternatives. Find a biological dentist that can assist you in this process. This may not be a quick step, as it will depend on the number of fillings that you have as well as your financial ability to do so, even if you have medical insurance. Start the process and diarize to have silver fillings replaced.

13. **Replace all plastic food containers with glass containers.**

    Plastic containers are not good for us to use, even the BPA-free ones. When storing food prior to or after cooking, change to glass or ceramic containers to store your food in. I like square or rectangular containers, as they fit better in the fridge than round ones. Glass mason jars are also great for storing soups and stews and pre-made salads in layers to take with you to work for your lunch!

14. **Replace plastic cooking utensils with bamboo, wood, food-grade silicone and stainless-steel cooking utensils.**

    Plastic utensils can leach chemicals into food when you use them in cooking. If pots and pans are on high heat, they can melt the plastic and plastic particles and toxins can leach into your food. Replace those utensils with wood, bamboo or stainless-steel alternatives. Start with a set of wooden spoons in different sizes and spatulas in bamboo or stainless steel if you have cast iron cookware. Stainless steel is a good option for ladles, whisks, potato mashers and graters. Have a large measuring cup in glass, and a set of measuring cups and spoons in stainless steel. Tongs with food-grade silicon tips are also a good addition to your kitchen toolset.

15. **Replace plastic cutting boards with glass, wood or bamboo cutting boards.**

    Glass cutting boards are the most hygienic, but not the most practical when you have kids. Unvarnished wood and bamboo boards are best for your knives.

16. **Replace Teflon-coated pots and pans.**

    While Teflon-coated cookware is easy to clean, relatively cheap and readily available, it is not the healthiest option. The problem is that Teflon releases toxic compounds when heated that leach into your food.

    Replacing your Teflon cookware all at once can be an expensive exercise, especially if you have a few pots and pans that you have bought over time. If you cannot replace all your pots and pans today, start with buying one pot or pan that you can use immediately. We do a lot of cooking on our stove, so I started with buying one large frying pan that I use almost every day. Then you can replace your cookware one-by-one as your budget allows. When you go shopping for new cookware, I recommend you consider carbon steel, cast iron and stainless steel cookware.

17. **Replace plastic wrap used for covering food with beeswax wraps.**

    Plastic wrap is very useful, but it is still plastic. Replace your plastic wrap with a better alternative: beeswax wraps or waxed paper works well to wrap food in to prevent it from drying out.

18. Replace aluminum used in cooking with chlorine-free parchment paper.

Aluminum and tinfoil are common for most of us, especially if you want to roast a delicious meat in the oven. What do we do? Cover it with tinfoil. Many prepared roasts that you find in the shops are placed in aluminum roasting pans, as it is relatively cheap, and conducts heat well. The problem with aluminum is that when it is heated, it seeps chemicals into the food. Aluminum is especially reactive to acidic foods like tomatoes. You can replace aluminum with the following alternatives:

- Cast iron is my favorite, especially the enamel-coated cast iron. Enamel-coated cast iron is easy to clean, which is the reason why I love it! It retains heat well, and it looks pretty when you want to serve your roast straight from the pan. You can find beautiful enameled cast iron skillets with lids that you can use in the oven!
- Stoneware is a fire-treated clay which looks beautiful on the table – you can take the cookware straight from the oven to the table! You can even use it to bake puddings and cakes, but at the time of writing this book, I haven't used stoneware, so this recommendation is based on the manufacturer's claims. You can find beautiful casserole dishes with lids that you can use in the oven.
- Glass is also an option to use in the oven. I often use glass roasters for meat and vegetables.

- Stainless steel is also an option, but remember to make sure it is not scratched, has rust or worn out, as you don't want the metals like nickel and copper leaching into your food.
- If you are grilling vegetables on the barbeque (or braai if you are South African), instead of using aluminum on the fire, use a stainless-steel grill basket or a Himalayan salt plate.

19. **Replace your body moisturizer, face wash, body wash and face moisturizer with non-toxic alternatives.**

Your skin is the largest organ in your body, and what you put on your skin is directly absorbed into the body without going through the liver. Your personal skin care products can have a huge impact on the toxic load in your body, so do your research and upgrade your moisturizers and washes to low or non-toxic alternatives.

20. **Add air-purifying plants to your home, and/or buy an air purifier to help clean the air.**

While you cannot clean the air outside your home, you can do a lot to clean the house in your home. Air-purifying plants are great at reducing toxins in your home. Some of the important toxins that plants can help clear are benzene (found in cigarette smoke, detergents and pesticides), formaldehyde (off-gassing from paints, solvents and other synthetic materials), trichloroethylene (in solvents) and xylene (found in varnishes, paints and paint thinners). If plants are not your thing or you are not home enough to keep them happy, another option is to get an air purifier. I would highly recommend you get an air purifier for your bedroom to clear airborne toxins. Air purifiers trap a high percentage of airborne allergen and irritants, like dust, VOCs, smoke and pollen. There is a wide range of air purifiers available, with different styles and at different prices.

21. Replace kitchen cleaner with a non-toxic alternative.

Store-bought kitchen cleaners are full of chemicals. You can purchase non-toxic kitchen cleaners at a health shop, or better still, make your own! Mix the following together in a spray bottle and shake to combine it: ½ cup white vinegar, ½ cup vodka, 1 and ½ cups water, 10 drops lavender essential oil and 10 drops lemon essential oil. Spray the surface, wait for 10 minutes to disinfect before wiping.

22. Support the natural detoxing pathways with activated charcoal.

Activated charcoal collects and holds chemicals that have a positive charge, including BPA, common pesticides, aflatoxin and other polar mycotoxins. When you take this, it is important to remember that it can bind the good vitamins and minerals as well! Therefore, don't take activated charcoal with any of your other supplements, including your thyroid hormone medication! Wait an hour after you have taken your thyroid hormone medication or any other supplements. You can take a couple of activated charcoal pills when you go for a sauna session or go exercising as it can then help to bind the toxins that your body will release during these sessions.

23. **Change cosmetics to less toxic or non-toxic cosmetics as far as possible.**

    Cosmetics are known to contain chemicals, many of them toxic to people who have Hashi's. Look at finding non-toxic alternatives for as many of the cosmetics that you are using as possible. You may need to do this over a period of time as cosmetics are expensive to replace. Do the best you can with as many cosmetic products as possible.

24. **Replace household cleaning products with non-toxic cleaning products.**

    Commercial household cleaning products have a huge amount of chemicals in them. Many traditional cleaning products contain harsh ingredients. These ingredients often have a negative impact on your hormones (endocrine disrupting), which can lead to weight gain, making you feel fatigued, lowering your thyroid function, and contribute to cancer growth. Some of the ingredients that are toxic are chlorine bleach, antibacterial ingredients like triclosan, formaldehyde, ammonia and fragrance (which include phthalates).

    You can replace these products with non-toxic cleaning products. The easiest option is to buy non-toxic cleaning products from a reputable online health retailer or your local health shop, or you can make your own. It is not difficult to make your own cleaning products using essential oils and general items like vinegar, bicarbonate of soda, lemon and salt. When you are using essential oils, specifically for cleaning, consider using lemongrass, eucalyptus, peppermint or orange essential oils, as these are all anti-bacterial.

25. Check for heavy metal toxicity

While all the actions leading to this point have been focusing on reducing the toxic load on your body and helping your body to detoxify naturally, there may still be instances where you may have been exposed to heavy metals and the body is not able to remove them effectively, or if you have had treatments like an MRI with contrast.

Consult with your doctor about testing for heavy metals toxicity. If you do have heavy metals present in your blood, your doctor will discuss treatment options with you. Treatment options may include intravenous (IV) glutathione treatment, as well as chelation therapy. Chelation therapy must be done under medical supervision, as there are risks involved.

CHAPTER 13: PILLAR 8 - MOVEMENT

Exercise is good for you! We know that. When you have Hashi's though, the way you exercise and what you would define as exercise, changes. You need to understand that forcing exercise when you are having a flare-up, when you don't even have the energy to get up in the morning, and when your thyroid is not optimal, can do you more harm than good. You don't want exercise to become the wrecking ball that destroys your health.

A number of years ago I was having a conversation with a doctor about feeling down and depressed. At this time I had not been diagnosed with Hashi's yet, and I was on the T4 hormone treatment for my underactive thyroid. I had no energy and had been gaining weight. The doctor's advice was that I should make an effort to exercise, as I would feel better afterwards. In hindsight, it was the worst advice a doctor could have given me. I tried to exercise, and my body just crashed. Instead of feeling better, I felt depleted and void. It took me three days of sleeping and resting to recover from one exercise session! That was not good advice! So let's look at what a healthy dose of exercise is, and what you should and shouldn't do when you have Hashi's.

When you feel good and have energy

The Physical Activity Guidelines issued by the U.S. Department of Health and Human Services recommends at least 150 minutes per week of moderate-intensity physical activity—think of it as 30 minutes, five days a week—for all adults, even the elderly and disabled.

The great thing about this is that you don't have to do all 30 minutes in a single daily session. In fact, the newest guidelines allow you to count all moderate intensity physical exertion throughout the day, even if it's just a few minutes at a time. You can do exercise in chunks: 10 or 15 minutes at a time, for example 10 minutes at breakfast, 10 minutes at lunch and 10 minutes in the late afternoon.

If you are already fit, you can cut your exercise time in half, to just 75 minutes a week for the health benefits, by doing vigorous exercise instead of moderate intensity. This means you can exercise 3 times a week for 25 minutes.

Exercise when you don't feel like it

When you do feel that you can exercise, don't push yourself too hard. People who have Hashi's can suffer from oxidative stress. Okay, here is a new term we need to understand. The body's cells produce free radicals during normal metabolic processes, as well as antioxidants that neutralize these free radicals. During this process, the body's balance is maintained between the antioxidants and the free radicals. Without going into detailed biology, here's what you need to know about free radicals. Free radicals can cause damage to the body when there is an excess. The free radicals can become unstable, and if this process continues, it begins a process called oxidative stress.

Physical activity, like exercise, can result in oxidative stress. Exercise increases free radical formation, which can cause the muscles to have temporary oxidative stress. It is temporary because the free radicals that are formed during physical activity regulate tissue growth as well as stimulate the production of antioxidants.

The body's immune system can also create free radicals for fighting off invading germs. These free radicals can damage healthy cells, which leads to inflammation. Once the immune system eliminates the infection or repairs the damaged tissue, the inflammation goes away.

However, we know that with Hashi's, the immune system is already working extremely hard. Modern life stressors also contribute to excess free radical production (including diet, lifestyle, certain conditions and environmental factors such as pollution and radiation), and the free radicals can become too much and deplete the antioxidant systems.

This is one of the many reasons why people who have Hashi's take longer to recover after exercise. It's not about eating more carbs or getting more rest. It's the burden of oxidative stress on the body that causes a longer recovery period.

Curb oxidative stress and free radicals: bring the antioxidants

To lessen the impact of free radicals and oxidative stress, you need antioxidants. The master antioxidant is glutathione. This little peptide plays a big role in how well you feel, how frequently you "crash" and how much of a struggle it is to lose weight with Hashi's.

Other antioxidants include vitamins A, C and E.

How can you increase glutathione and other antioxidants? First, eat a healthy and varied diet. While whey protein is something we could use as it contains antioxidants, we need to avoid this as it is a dairy product. Then, we can take supplements, specifically those that include n-acetyl cysteine (called NAC, a precursor to glutathione) or acetylated forms of glutathione.

When you don't have the energy

When there are days that you feel that you don't have any energy available to do any form of exercise, then don't. Remember that with hypothyroidism, your thyroid is not working as it is required to. When your thyroid hormones are running low, you are also at risk for tendinitis, pain and nagging injuries that refuse to heal. This is over above the in-your-bones exhaustion that you are feeling.

Exercises that other people can do and that seem reasonable to do, like spinning or high-repetition low-intensity strength training, can wreak havoc on you. Let's take a moment to talk about what exercise does when you are not in an optimal state.

Cortisol and exercise

First, we need to talk about cortisol. When you do high intensity or endurance exercise, your body releases glucocorticoids (cortisol, the fight-or-flight hormone) in response to the stress. In the short term, you may feel that it takes longer to recover between sets, and your resting heart rate may also be higher.

In the long term, if your cortisol is high all the time due to stress and exercise, it can lead to the exact things that you are trying to avoid by doing exercise in the first place: increased blood pressure, diabetes, weight gain, osteoporosis, and even impaired fertility. It can also increase hormones like testosterone and subsequently estrogen, while decreasing hormones like progesterone (which can cause disruptions in the menstrual cycle for women and cause acne).

The focus should rather be on recharging your batteries. Chris Kesser suggests the following 3-stage approach to exercise:

- *Stage One*: limit exercise to gentle activities, like walking, restorative yoga, tai chi or mild swimming or cycling.
- *Stage Two*: as you start to feel better, gradually add some more moderate exercises. Don't go too quickly, as you risk putting too much stress on your body and then putting yourself right back to where you where before you started.
- *Stage Three*: when you have rebuilt your energy, you are good to go to full exercise routines. It is still important to be careful and not to push too hard too quickly and relapse.

What to do when you don't feel you can exercise

Rest when you must, and then try to do something light and energizing, like going for a walk outside in nature. Keep it light and easy.

This is not an excuse for becoming a coach potato. It is a sign that you need to rest while you do all the other things that you need to do in order to get you up again, like making sure your thyroid hormones are optimal, eating food like sweet potatoes to add slow-release energy, including a glutathione or NAC supplement and managing the impact of stress in your life.

Action Steps

1. **Only exercise when you have energy.**

   While exercise is generally good for you, be careful of exercising too hard when you don't have energy or when you are experiencing an autoimmune flare-up. Take it slow and do gentle exercises. As your health and energy returns, you can turn it up and exercise for longer and more vigorously.

2. **Supplement with NAC or liposomal glutathione.**

   These supplements are antioxidants, which help to protect you against oxidative stress. When you take NAC, your body turns it into glutathione by binding it with alpha-lipoic acid, which helps protect you from metal damage

CHAPTER 14: PILLAR 9 - SUPPLEMENTS

Do you really need to supplement?

Targeted supplements are a great way to ensure you obtain the nutrients you need for your health. The food we eat today is not of the same quality as it was say, 50 or more years ago, due to commercialization of farming, the use of pesticides and eating genetically modified foodstuffs. Supplements can replace the vitamins and minerals that are not available in the food anymore. Another reason to use supplements is that the processing, transporting and storage of foods destroys nutrients.

Some people with certain medical conditions will benefit from taking supplements. Specific diets may also be void of certain nutrients as specific food groups are avoided, like vegetarianism and veganism, and specific diets to treat your hypothyroidism can also lead to nutrient depletion. Some medications can also deplete the body of nutrients, like acid blockers, antibiotics and synthetic estrogens and progesterones.

Many doctors, specialists, scientists, and people who have Hashi's, have researched the vitamins and minerals that are important for improving and maintaining good health. While I strongly believe that we should get most of the nutrients from our food, we can certainly benefit from appropriate supplements.

However, before we do that, a word of caution. Supplements are not drugs (medicine) and therefore they are unregulated. This also means that manufacturers do not need to test supplements for safety or effectiveness. Manufactures can make claims like "may improve weight loss" without having the scientific tests and scrutiny to back it up. Supplements from natural (plant or animal) sources should also be carefully considered. "Natural" does not necessarily mean "safe". Always do your research and make sure you understand what it is that you are putting into your body, and why you are taking it.

Always declare which supplements you are taking when you see your doctor. Even better, ask your doctor which supplements you should be taking, as well as when you should be taking them. Your doctor will be able to inform you which supplements to take, as well as the quality of the supplements they recommend. For example, when taking a magnesium supplement, you should not take it at the same time of the day as calcium and iron supplements, because they will impact the absorption of each other.

Two roles of supplements

There are two kinds of supplementation. Firstly, there are supplements to help maintain micronutrients in the body that may be difficult to find even in a healthy diet, for example vitamin D and vitamin A. Secondly, there are supplements that have therapeutic value and can help to accomplish a specific goal, for example helping with insomnia or reducing inflammation.

I am going to focus on the supplements for people who have Hashi's. Keep in mind that what works for some may not work for you, and vice versa. You need to review your symptoms and establish what works for you. This is also the reason why I don't believe a multi-vitamin is ideal – it's like just throwing something into your body and hoping that some of it will work for you. First of all, it's a waste of your money, and second, what is working for one person may actually be detrimental to another! Supplements need to be specific to your needs, and with Hashi's, we have very specific needs.

There are the nutrients that are helpful in keeping you healthy, and then there are specific nutrients that can help when you are experiencing a flare-up. Ideally, you want to obtain these nutrients from your diet, but if you cannot obtain these nutrients through food, it is time to consider the addition of a supplement. Firstly, let's look at the "regular" supplements, listed alphabetically:

1. Betaine with pepsin
2. Ferritin
3. Magnesium
4. Omega 3
5. Selenium
6. Vitamin B1 (Thiamine)
7. Vitamin B12
8. Vitamin D

9. Vitamin E
10. Zinc

BETAINE WITH PEPSIN

When you have Hashi's, it is very likely that you have low stomach acid. This will have an impact on your ability to digest protein and fats, and betaine can help with this.

Betaine, also known as trimethylclycine, is an amino acid which not only helps with digestion, but also helps with liver function and detoxification. It is commonly found in wheat products, and because we should avoid wheat products, we may struggle with low stomach acid. It is for this reason that betaine is recommended, even though the studies on this amino acid are limited. Even better, betaine HCI (hydrochloric acid) is a good choice if you are worried about low stomach acid.

When you are looking for this supplement, look for one that has added pepsin. Pepsin is another little wonder enzyme which helps to break protein into smaller pieces so that it can be properly and easily absorbed by the small intestine.

There isn't a recommended dosage for taking betaine with pepsin, so you will need to experiment to find the right dosage for you. Take one capsule with a protein meal. If you feel a burning sensation in your throat, you don't need the supplement or there wasn't enough protein in the meal. If you didn't feel anything, increase your dosage by one capsule with your next protein-included meal. Keep increasing the dosage per protein-included meal until you feel the discomfort or burning sensation in your throat. Then you know you have found the right dosage, minus the last increase. So, if you feel any discomfort at three capsules, you now know that you need to only take two capsules when you eat a meal with protein in it.

FERRITIN

People with Hashi's have been associated with low levels of ferritin. While we often link fatigue to low iron levels, we also need to look at ferritin, which is the protein in which iron is stored. You want to do both a ferritin and iron level blood test, as the combination of the two tells you a story. While the iron test reveals the amount of iron that is in the blood available for use, the ferritin level tells you the iron that is stored for later use.

If your ferritin is low, it indicates that your iron storage is low and that you could have an iron deficiency. If your iron is low, this can be due to a vitamin B12 or a folate deficiency. If ferritin is too high, it may indicate an iron storage disorder such as hemochromatosis. It is also possible to have high levels of ferritin with low levels of iron. Research has shown that ferritin is also an acute phase reactant (meaning that ferritin may increase when there is inflammation). Some people may have high ferritin levels due to inflammation but low iron levels due to some deficiency.

MAGNESIUM

Magnesium is called the mighty mineral. It is an essential mineral and an electrolyte, and it is required in more than 300 biochemical reactions in the body. It supports the immune system, helps to maintain normal nerve and muscle function, keeps blood glucose levels stable and helps with energy production. With Hashi's, we are at risk of having a magnesium deficiency, and exposure to toxins (like fluoride and alcohol) doesn't help.

Most of us will benefit from taking a magnesium supplement. However, there is more to this than just simply taking magnesium. There are different forms of magnesium, and you need to find the one that will work best for your body:

- Magnesium chloride is extracted from brine or ocean water and is argued to be the most effective form of magnesium. It encourages sleep, digestion, both health and a sense of calm. The key side effect is that it can also cause diarrhea.
- Magnesium sulphate is also known as Epsom salts, and well known by athletes or anyone with sore muscles. This form is also very well known for its laxative effects.
- Magnesium citrate is derived from citric acid and has excellent bioavailability. This can be used to support digestion naturally (to relieve constipation and acid indigestion). It may lead to dehydration as it pulls water into the intestines and can lead to an imbalance of minerals in the body.
- Magnesium oxide is found in Milk of Magnesia and similar products which organically encourages improved digestion. This form of magnesium has a lower bioavailability (only 4 percent) compared to magnesium citrate (at 90 percent).

- Magnesium glycinate is one of the best forms of magnesium if you are feeling stressed. This form is the best one of all the magnesium forms to naturally support muscle relaxation. It has optimum bioavailability, and best of all, it is not known for its laxative effect. As a side note, the amino acid glycine is known for its calming impact on the body and mind. This form can worsen anxiety symptoms, so if you are anxious, rather consider magnesium citrate.
- Magnesium orotate is great at promoting heart health. It includes orotic acid (previously known as B13) and it is a favorite with athletes as it helps with the repair process of tissues, enhances stamina and improves performance. This form of magnesium is also more expensive compared to the other forms of magnesium.
- Magnesium L-threonate is considered the "breakthrough" supplement by some people. It has good bioavailability, and it also has the potential to improve cognitive functions. It may sharpen your wit and ability to remember information.

Some forms of minerals are labelled as "chelated". These are minerals which have been chemically combined with amino acids to form "complexes". These are marketed as minerals which have a higher bioavailability compared to non-chelated minerals, but there is very little scientific evidence to support this claim.

Ideally, you want to take magnesium before bedtime. Also, don't take magnesium at the same time of the day you are taking your thyroid hormones or iron/calcium supplements, as magnesium blocks their absorption. So if you are taking your thyroid hormones in the morning, you can take your magnesium in the afternoon or evening.

People with reduced renal functions are at risk of magnesium toxicity and should avoid high-dose supplements.

OMEGA-3

Omega-3 is an essential fatty acid, which means that the body cannot produce it and we have to make sure that we take enough of it in through our food. Food such as oily fish, chia seeds, walnuts, wild rice and flaxseeds are high in omega-3. While seafood is a great source of omega-3, a lot of seafood also contains heavy metal toxins. So, if you look at eating fish, keep to the cold water fatty fish like salmon, anchovies, herring, trout and Pacific or Atlantic mackerel. One of the great benefits of omega-3 is that it is anti-inflammatory and can even stop inflammation from occurring.

So, this is something that you should consider taking every day. Look for a high-quality fish oil which contains both EPA and DPA (two types of omega-3). However, a word of warning – if you are taking blood thinners such as warfarin, or if you have a bleeding disorder, please speak to your doctor first before you start supplementing with omega-3.

SELENIUM

Selenium is a powerful antioxidant and plays a key role in metabolism. It also helps to detoxify the body from heavy metals like lead and mercury. Some studies have also found it beneficial in thyroid hormone production and converting T4 hormones to T3 hormones.

If you have a deficiency in selenium, you will likely experience anxiety, fatigue and depression. I recommend that you take a selenium supplement for a period of at least three months. This is however something you don't want to overdose on, as you can become toxic from it, causing gastrointestinal illness, hair loss and nail discoloration. You can also experience muscle or joint pain, headaches, foul breath, fatigue/weakness, or a skin reaction. Should this happen, stop taking selenium and consult with your doctor.

VITAMIN B1 (THIAMINE)

Thiamine, known as vitamin B1, is responsible for converting carbohydrates into energy, and it also helps with the digestion of proteins and fats. Thiamine can also help to release more stomach acid, aiding in protein digestion.

There are two different forms of vitamin B1, namely thiamine and benfotiamine. It is important that you take the right one. Thiamine is water-soluble, which means that whatever the body is not absorbing, is excreted through urine. Benfotiamine is fat-soluble, which means that the body does not excrete any excess, and you risk overdosing on it, which can make you ill. So in summary, while benfotiamine has better bioavailability, it is safer to supplement with the water-soluble thiamine.

VITAMIN B12

Vitamin B12 is an essential vitamin that is required to produce red blood cells and DNA, and this also aids in digestion. You don't need a large amount of it, but you do need to replenish it every day. As we grow older, we become at risk of being deficient due to less stomach acid needed to convert vitamin B12 effectively. This vitamin is also water-soluble, so any excess will just be flushed out of the body by the kidneys.

According to a study in 2007 done by the Experiential Biology and Medicine group, vitamin B12 is difficult to absorb. They found that the vitamin B12 in animal protein was the most absorbable, while the vitamin B12 in eggs was somewhat poorly absorbed. Even the "superfood" algae foods, such as blue-green algae was not very absorbable at all.

What should you do if you want to supplement with vitamin B12? While there are four types of vitamin B12, it doesn't really matter which form you take – there isn't any research yet that indicates the use of one form over the other with regards to bioavailability or absorption. Vitamin B12 as a dietary supplement is usually in the form of cyanocobalamin, and can also contain methylcobalamin and other forms of vitamin B12.

Vitamin B12 can be increased by having vitamin B12 injections and this is also available as sublingual (under the tongue) preparations. It just depends on which option you prefer.

VITAMIN D3

Most people with Hashi's are deficient in vitamin D. This nutrient is not really a vitamin, as it acts more like a hormone than a vitamin. It is fat-soluble, which means you need a blood test to check your levels, as an overdose can cause health issues.

You want your vitamin D level to be optimum, meaning that it is between 50-80 ng/ml (nanograms per milliliter). The benefit of vitamin D is that it helps to reduce thyroid antibodies for people who are taking levothyroxine (synthetic thyroid hormones). Low levels of vitamin D are related to heart disease, autoimmune disease, depression, and more recently, thyroid conditions.

To increase your levels of vitamin D, the first and best source is to get some sunshine on your skin! If you are unable to find the time to be in the sun or live in a country where sunshine is limited, it is highly recommended that you supplement with vitamin D. You can also look at blue light therapy to mimic the exposure to the sun.

When you speak to your doctor about a vitamin D supplement, ask for cholecalciferol. This form of vitamin D is the most bioavailable, compared to vitamin D2 (called ergocalciferol).

VITAMIN E

Vitamin E is a powerful antioxidant and plays an important role in the immune system, and it is for this reason that we look at it. Vitamin E also works with selenium in the process to convert T4 hormones to T3 hormones.

While vitamin E is fat-soluble, there is currently no reliable test to provide accurate results of vitamin E levels in your blood. So, stick to a daily dosage of 268 gm. Be careful not to overdose on vitamin E – bleeding or easy bruising is a sign that you might be taking too much.

There are different types of vitamin E used in supplements, which are broken in two groups: tocopherols and tocotrienols (of which there are four types of each). Many vitamin E supplements only have alpha tocopherol in, which is limited, and you would want to at least buy a supplement which has mixed tocopherols. The best option is a whole food vitamin E complex, which will contain both totopherols and tocotrienols.

ZINC

Zinc is a trace element, a type of metal, which is anti-inflammatory, and that is why it is included here. It also helps to maintain health and performs important functions, like helping with hormone production (and for us, specifically thyroid hormones), improves immunity and facilitates digestion. Another benefit of zinc is that it helps the body in the detoxing process.

If you are deficient in zinc, this can impact the conversation of T4 to T3 hormones. Zinc is also needed to form TSH. People who are at risk for being deficient include those who are vegan, vegetarian, or struggle from digestive issues or severe stomach-acid issues. Woman who take the birth-control pill or who are on hormone replacement therapy may also be at risk from lower levels of zinc. Stress and certain medications can also impact zinc levels.

While there are different forms of zinc (zinc picolinate, zinc gluconate, zinc sulphate, zinc orotate, zinc citrate and zinc acetate) it doesn't seem to matter which one you take. At the time of publishing, there is little science to prove any significant differences between these forms or that one form is superior to another form. Some research suggests that zinc picolinate appears to be better absorbed than the other types of zinc.

A word of warning: zinc supplementation can lead to a depletion in iron levels. If you suspect a deficiency in zinc, speak to your doctor about checking the levels with a blood test. It is also possible that a zinc deficiency can lead to a copper deficiency.

Specific supplements when you have a flare-up

When you have a flare-up or worsening of your Hashi's symptoms, you are very likely experiencing inflammation. To help with the inflammation, I recommend the following supplements, listed alphabetically:

1. Bromelain
2. Curcumin.
3. Glutathione or NAC
4. Vitamin A
5. Vitamin C

BROMELAIN

The humble pineapple has been used in traditional medicine since ancient times. Pineapples have an enzyme called bromelain, which can help to reduce inflammation. It also has other health benefits, including antithrombotic and fibrinolytic affects, anti-cancer activity and immunomodulatory effects, helping to reduce soreness in muscles and helping wounds heal. When you combine it with turmeric, you can increase the effects of bromelain.

You can find various forms of bromelain as a supplement, including powder, cream, tablets or capsules. If you want the benefits that bromelain offers, it won't be enough to eat pineapple or drink the juice, you will have to take a supplement for it to be effective.

CURCUMIN

Curcumin is often confused with turmeric. Turmeric is a spice that is used in cooking, while curcumin is the key active ingredient in turmeric, which is an anti-inflammatory antioxidant. While incorporating turmeric in your cooking is great, it may be worthwhile to take a curcumin supplement to boost the benefits that curcumin offers.

If you are going to use turmeric in your cooking, always use it with saturated fat. Curcumin is insoluble in water, but soluble in fat. You can find saturated fats in the fatty cuts of beef, pork, and lamb, and in coconut oil, coconut milk and cream. Black pepper also aids in the bioavailability of curcumin, as it contains peperine that helps with the absorption of curcumin. Research has shown that just by adding black pepper with curcumin, the bioavailability increases by 2000%.

If you have an iron deficiency, curcumin may interfere with the way the body absorbs iron. Also, avoid curcumin and turmeric if you are taking blood thinning mediation.

GLUTATHIONE or NAC (N-Acetyl Cysteine)

NAC is a great little worker against the damage of free radicals, meaning it is a powerful antioxidant. When you take NAC, your body turns it into glutathione by binding it with alpha-lipoic acid, which helps protect you from metal damage (according to studies in human and rat cells). Glutathione also supports the liver enzymes that break down mold toxins and heavy metals. You can also take a supplement for glutathione, and make sure it is *liposomal glutathione*, as your digestive system will destroy normal glutathione in supplements.

Another very useful benefit of NAC is that when you have mucus in your nose or throat, NAC can help to thin it out. Take NAC with the anti-inflammatory bromelain (which is sourced from pineapple stems) to see a quick improvement.

VITAMIN A

Vitamin A is not just important for eye health! It also helps with the immune system and cell growth. While other nutrients are important for thyroid health, it is interesting to note that in this case, thyroid hormones play an important role in converting beta-carotene into vitamin A! People with Hashi's are often deficient in vitamin A for this reason. Blood tests to check for vitamin A levels are not reliable, so it is more difficult to determine if someone is deficient in vitamin A. A histological examination of the conjunctiva in the eye could indicate a deficiency, as well as lesions on the skin and night blindness.

This vitamin is also fat-soluble, which means that what you absorb stays in the body, and there is always a risk of overdosing.

VITAMIN C

You have probably heard many times that when you are starting to experience the symptoms of a cold, to start increasing your dosage of vitamin C. This water-soluble vitamin is a powerful antioxidant, as it protects the body against oxidative stress and therefore plays an important role in helping to prevent disease. What is the dosage that can help you with this? Well, eating a healthy diet with foods that contain vitamin C, and supplementing with 500 mg twice day is all you need to help to alleviate inflammatory markers.

Our bodies cannot make vitamin C, so it is very important that we eat foods that contain vitamin C. When you are looking for vitamin C, you may find it as L-ascorbic acid. If you don't get enough vitamin C, you are at risk to develop scurvy, the symptoms of which include fatigue and overall connective tissue weakness. The ideal is to get your daily dosage of vitamin C through your diet, by eating foods such as raw sweet red peppers, oranges, and broccoli.

When you are looking at a vitamin C supplement, you may find that there are different names under which vitamin C is better known:

ascorbic acid, sodium ascorbate, calcium ascorbate, ascorbic acid with bioflavonoids, and combination products which contain calcium ascorbate, dehydroascorbate, calcium thionate, xylonate and lyxonate. Does it matter which one you take? Research shows that there are some differences in uptake between the different forms, but the plain and simple form of ascorbic acid is preferred due to the relatively low cost of ascorbic acid.

So how much should you take? Research indicates that a moderate intake of 30 to 180 mg a day is absorbed approximately 70% to 90%. When you take more than 1 gram a day, the absorption falls to less than 50% absorbed, and the body excretes the remaining unmetabolized ascorbic acid.

While vitamin C has low toxicity, if you take too much, it may cause diarrhea, nausea, and abdominal cramps. There is conflicting evidence that high doses of vitamin C cause kidney stones, unless you have pre-existing hyperoxaluria. Also, people who have hereditary hemochromatosis, could have an iron overload and resulting tissue damage when taking high doses of vitamin C.

Quick Reference Guide

The table below provides a quick summary of the nutrients, and it also lists the food sources and dosage if you are going to supplement with it.

Nutrient	Information	Food Sources	Dosage
Betaine with pepsin	Amino acid that supports liver function, aids digestion, process fats.	Beets, spinach, sweet potato, turkey breast, veal and beef.	Start with one capsule on empty stomach before each meal, build up until optimal dosage.
Ferritin	Needed for iron storage. Blood test required to check levels, check iron levels as well.	Meat (red meat, liver, poultry), seafood (fish, oysters), and spinach.	As per doctor's advice. Avoid taking within 2-4 hours of thyroid hormones
Magnesium	Essential mineral and electrolyte, support immune system and energy production	Spinach, dry roasted cashews or almonds, avocado, banana, salmon, chicken breast, beef, broccoli, apple and carrot.	100-400 mg daily, take it at bedtime.
Omega 3	Anti-inflammatory helps to lower blood pressure, positive impact on cholesterol.	Oily fish, chia seeds, walnuts, wild rice and flaxseeds.	One to four grams per day, with meals.
Selenium	Antioxidant, supports thyroid hormone conversion, helps with fatigue and depression.	Nuts (like brazil and walnuts), many fresh and saltwater fish, beef and poultry.	200-400 mcg per day, taken for a period of 3 months to 2 years. If you have a reaction, may have iron deficiency.

Nutrient	Information	Food Sources	Dosage
Vit B1 (Thiamine)	Aids digestion of protein and fats by helping release of stomach acid. Avoid fat-soluble version (benfotiamine).	Meat (pork, turkey, chicken, beef), seafood (trout, mussels, tuna, salmon), acorn squash, orange juice, toasted sunflower seeds.	600 mg per day can turn around fatigue in 3 to 5 days. Period to take: 3 months to 2 years.
Vit B12	Needed to produce red-blood cells and DNA, aids digestion, maintain energy levels. Best absorbed from animal protein.	Grass-fed meat, organ meats, fish and seafood and egg yolk.	5000 mcg sublingually (under the tongue) daily for 10 days; then 5000 mcg, once per week, for 4 weeks; then 5000 mcg monthly for maintenance.
Vit D3	Helps body to absorb calcium, plays role in immune system, help to reduce thyroid antibodies. Blood test required to check levels.	Cod liver oil, fish (swordfish, salmon, tuna, sardines), beef liver and egg yolk, but it is often not enough. Best way is sun exposure, and the alternative is blue light therapy.	As per doctor's advice, need blood serum levels to be 50-80 n/mg. Consult with your doctor.
Vit E	Antioxidant which supports conversion of T4 to T3. Avoid supplements if you are undergoing chemotherapy or radiation therapy, or if you are on a blood thinner.	Green leafy vegetables, eggs, nuts, and some through meat.	Daily dose of 268 gm. Take with selenium to ensure proper absorption.

Nutrient	Information	Food Sources	Dosage
Zinc	Anti-inflammatory, helps with hormone production, improves immunity, aids digestion.	Animal protein, including lamb, grass-fed beef, poultry, eggs, mushrooms, salmon, cacao powder and pumpkin seeds.	30 mg a day, with 40 mg a day as the upper limit (above 40 mg may cause a deficiency in copper levels), taken with food.
When you experience a flare up			
Bromelain	Reduces inflammation and immunomodulatory effects, reduces soreness in muscles and helps wounds heal.	Pineapple (but not enough bromelain in it for therapeutic value, need to supplement).	80 to 400 milligrams per serving, two to three times daily. Discuss with your doctor before taking it.
Curcumin	Anti-inflammatory, antioxidant, anti-microbial, anti-thrombotic. Buy a supplement that has been tested and is proven to be well-absorbed, and is combined with piperine. Always check the filler ingredients as well (avoid the supplements with wheat, barley, rye, and some that even contains lead and food colorant called metanil yellow).	Turmeric.	Seems to be safe up to 8 grams per day.

Nutrient	Information	Food Sources	Dosage
Glutathione or NAC	Helps to prevent free radical damage, can help to heal intestinal permeability (leaky gut). Can be in supplement form or as prescription drug.	None.	As supplement, no recommend dosages are available. Always take with food.
Vitamin A	Anti-inflammatory, necessary for eye health.	Fish (cod, salmon, halibut), liver, beef, chicken, eggs, carrots, spinach, sweet potatoes and cantaloupe.	Can be toxic in large dosages. Consult with your doctor.
Vitamin C	Helps with biosynthesis of collagen, L-carnitine and certain neurotransmitters, it is involved in protein metabolism, an antioxidant, regenerates other antioxidants in the body, like vitamin E, and limits the damaging effects of free radicals.	Raw sweet red or green pepper, guava, orange, kiwi fruit, broccoli, strawberries, brussel sprouts, grapefruit, cantaloupe, cabbage, cauliflower, potato, tomato, spinach, green peas, kale, lemon juice.	More than 600 mg a day for therapeutic value.

Action Steps

1. **Check vitamin D and ferritin levels before you supplement with them.**

   Ask your functional doctor to test the vitamin D and ferritin levels in your blood. Vitamin D plays an important role in immune function and helps to reduce thyroid antibodies, while ferritin is needed for iron storage. Speak with your functional doctor about supplementation options and dosages, as these nutrients will be stored in your body and you don't want to risk overdosing.

2. **Drink magnesium daily.**

   Magnesium helps your body in the detoxing process. There are different forms of magnesium, so you will need to find a supplement that works for you. If you drink your thyroid hormones in the morning, I recommend you take magnesium in the afternoon or evening. Also, don't take iron and calcium supplements at the same time of the day as magnesium, as magnesium blocks the absorption of iron and calcium.

3. **Increase omega-3, selenium, vitamin B12 and zinc with food or supplements.**

   Most people with Hashi's are deficient in these nutrients. While food does provide certain amounts of nutrients to the body, to get the benefit of these nutrients you may also consider high-quality supplements.

- Selenium helps to eliminate heavy metals, and some studies have also shown that it helps with thyroid hormone production and conversation from T4 to T3. Take 200-400 mcg per day, for a period of 3 months to 2 years.
- Zinc is an important trace element, as it is a strong antioxidant and helps to remove toxins, particularly heavy metals, from your body. Start taking a zinc supplement every day with food: 30 mg per day, and not more than 40mg per day (as it can lead to a deficiency in copper). Avoid the intranasal zinc sprays.
- Vitamin B12 is an essential vitamin required to produce red blood cells and DNA, and it also aids in digestion. It is water-soluble so any excess B12 will be excreted.
- Omega-3 is an antioxidant and anti-inflammatory and helps to correct the balance between the omega-3/omega-6. Take one to four grams per day, with meals. I recommend getting a high-quality oil with both EPA and DPA.

4. **Supplement with glutathione or NAC.**

   Glutathione is a powerful antioxidant that protects you from heavy metal damage and supports the liver. It is not available through food sources. You can take NAC (N-Acetyl Cysteine) and your body will build glutathione on its own, or you can take a glutathione supplement, specifically liposomal glutathione.

5. **Supplement with Betaine with pepsin and vitamin B1 (thiamine).**

   Betaine with pepsin helps in addressing low stomach acid, something that many Hashi's sufferers have. Vitamin B1, specifically in thiamine form, also helps with protein digestion.

A FINAL WORD

The actions listed here are what I would recommend when you start on your healing journey. My aim is to make it as easy as possible to introduce the changes in just about every aspect of your life – what you eat, how you prepare your food, ensuring you have optimum nutrition and making the lifestyle changes to manage stress and sleep better.

You don't have to do all the actions I have listed here in the order that I have documented them. You can change the order of actions to best suit your life and circumstances.

These are also not the only actions you can take. As research on autoimmunity is completed and published, and we see advancements in technology and medical breakthroughs, what we can do to improve our health may change or there may be additional actions we can take. Please don't see this book and the actions here as the "everything-you-need-know book", as what we know may change. This is my guideline based on many years of experience, written in the hope that you will benefit from my trial and errors along the way.

Always remember this: Do your research. You are your own best advocate – don't let any doctor tell you it is all in your head. There is no one right way – do what works for you. If you fall off the wagon, be kind to yourself and catch that wagon again. Be kind to yourself always. Take each day, day by day. This is the start of your journey to attain better health and an enjoyable lifestyle. I have achieved this and you can too.

How I can help you

So, that is the story. This entire book is what I would have liked to have learned at the time I was first diagnosed with Hashimoto's Thyroiditis. While the book is here to assist you in gaining knowledge and to arm you with insight to act, you may need guidance and support on your own health journey. It gives me the opportunity and the pleasure to provide you with a few excellent add-on services to help supplement this book.

- Individual coaching and support
- Workshops and retreats
- Keynote talks
- Online course

I would love to hear from you and learn about your successes in your journey. Let's stay in touch! You can connect with me on social media and by visiting my website.

- Instagram: @adeledurand and @healthyhashihacks
- Website: www.adeledurand.com
- Email: hashis@adeledurand.com

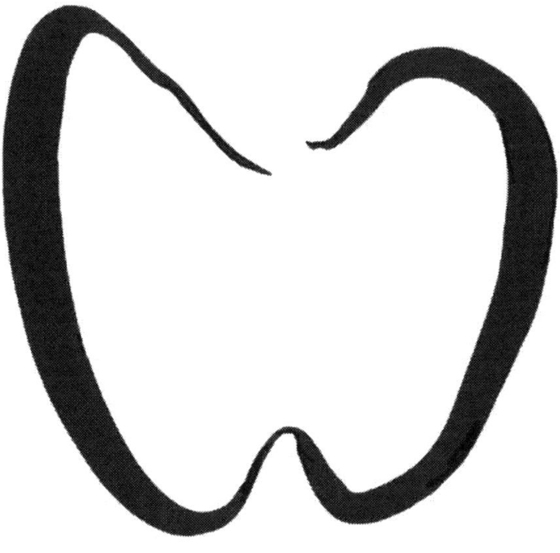

GRATITUDE

I'd like to give special mention to the people who supported me in my healing journey, as well as in helping me to write this book.

First and foremost, my husband Johann, who supports me in every endeavor and project I pursue, and who takes care of me when I am unable to take care of myself. You are my biggest cheerleader, and I love you!

My beautiful daughter Jeanine, who accepts me as I am. Keep on believing that you can make the world a better place. Thank you for choosing me to be your mum. I love you.

My best friend Janet, we have been friends since our first year at university when we car pooled together. We have been each other's support on our respective healing journeys. Thank you for being there for me and encouraging me to write this book.

My friend Sarah. You are an inspiration as a friend and a mum! I remember the day at the spa when we committed to writing our books. Thanks for your support and continuous reminders to get it done!

A special mention to Nikki Bush. You are an inspiration as a mom, wife and friend. A talented professional speaker and author. Thank you for your support and encouragement!

To the members of the Hashimoto's South Africa Facebook group, a huge shout-out and thank you! I have learned so much from you. You share your insights and experiences, and your courage to take back your health inspires me every day. You are brave and strong, and I admire you. You unknowingly motivated me to write this book.

To the amazing doctors and researchers who fight the good fight for better health, and who publish and share their knowledge, thank you! You have helped me in my healing journey, and your passion and dedication give hope to so many. I have tried my best to give credit and reference your work in this book and the bibliography. Thank you for your hard work, dedication and willingness to help others.

Lastly, my friends who have been with me in the Mastermind group since April 2020 – Jason, Carl, Chris and Rodger. You have been a voice of support and reasoning in the crazy time of lockdown due to Covid-19. Our daily online meetings are invaluable. You share knowledge, insight and jokes, and have become true friends. Thank you!

BIBLIOGRAPHY

8Fit. n.d. *What Are Macronutrients and Why Are They Important.* Accessed February 2, 2020. https://8fit.com/nutrition/what-are-macronutrients-and-why-are-they-important/.

Almekinder, Elisabeth. n.d. *6 Ways to Improve Gut Health.* Accessed April 22, 2020. https://www.bluezones.com/2019/04/6-ways-to-improve-gut-health/.

American Thyroid Association. 2013. *Desiccated thyroid extract vs Levothyroxine in the treatment of hypothyroidism.* March. Accessed November 20, 2019. https://www.thyroid.org/patient-thyroid-information/ct-for-patients/vol-6-issue-8/vol-6-issue-8-p-3/.

—. n.d. *Thyroid Function Tests.* Accessed November 24, 2019. https://www.thyroid.org/thyroid-function-tests/.

Anderson, Paul. 2013. *Epigenetics.* March 5. Accessed December 6, 2019. https://www.youtube.com/watch?v=i9a-ru2ES6Y.

Asprey, Dave. n.d. *8 Detox methods that work really well.* Accessed May 29, 2020. https://daveasprey.com/7-detox-methods-that-really-work/.

—. 2016. *The complete bulletproof guide do gluten and grains .* December 1. Accessed January 6, 2020.

https://www.bulletproof.com/diet/bulletproof-diet/the-complete-bulletproof-guide-to-grains/.

—. n.d. *The Science Behind Just One Mold Toxin in your Coffee.* Accessed May 29, 2020. https://daveasprey.com/one-ugly-mug-the-science-behind-just-one-mold-toxin-in-your-coffee/.

—. n.d. *What to Eat When You Have Autoimmune Disease.* Accessed January 6, 2020. https://daveasprey.com/autoimmune-disease-diet/.

Atkins. n.d. *10 Reasons Why Sugar Is Bad for Your Health.* Accessed January 9, 2020. https://www.atkins.com/how-it-works/library/articles/10-ways-sugar-harms-your-health.

Atkuri, Kondala R, John J Mantovani, Leonard A Herzenberg, and Leonore A Herzenberg. 2007. *N-acetylcysteine - a safe antidote for cysteine/glutathione deficiency.* June 29. Accessed May 18, 2020. https://www.ncbi.nlm.nih.gov/pmc/articles/PMC4540061/.

Axe, Josh. 2018. *Top 7 Essential Oils for Anxiety.* March 9. Accessed March 6, 2020. https://draxe.com/essential-oils/essential-oils-for-anxiety/.

Barrell, Amanda. 2018. *The best carrier oils for essential oils.* April 26. Accessed March 7, 2020. https://www.medicalnewstoday.com/articles/321639.

Bautista-Toledo, I, M.A. Ferro-Carcia, J Rivera-Utrilla, C Moreno-Castilla, and F.J. Vegas Fernández. 2005. *Bisphenol A Removal from Water by Activated Carbon. Effects of Carbon Characteristics and Solution Chemistry.* July 9. Accessed April 6, 2020. https://pubs.acs.org/doi/abs/10.1021/es0481169.

Becker, Alan, and Karam F.A. Soliman. 2009. *The Role of Intracellular Glutathione in Inorganic Mercury-Induced Toxicity in Neuroblastoma Cells.* April 4. Accessed May 20, 2020. https://www.ncbi.nlm.nih.gov/pmc/articles/PMC2882944/.

Bells, Becky. 2017. *Is Leaky Gut Syndrome a Real Condition? An Unbiased Look.* February 2. Accessed December 12, 2019. https://www.healthline.com/nutrition/is-leaky-gut-real.

Bischoff, Stephan C, Biovanni Barbara, Wim Buurman, Theo Ockhuizen, Jörg-Dieter Schulzke, Matteo Serino, Herbert Tilg, Alastair Watson, and Jerry M Wells. 2014. *Intestinal permeability – a new target for disease prevention and therapy.* November 18. Accessed January 15, 2020. https://www.ncbi.nlm.nih.gov/pmc/articles/PMC4253991/.

Bishnoi, A, H.E. Carlson, B.L. Gruber, L.D. Kaufman, J.L. Bock, and K Lidonnici. 1994. *Effects of commonly prescribed nonsteroidal anti-inflammatory drugs on thyroid hormone measurements.* March. Accessed April 10, 2020. https://pubmed.ncbi.nlm.nih.gov/8154511/.

Blewitt, Marnie, and Emma Whitelaw. 2013. *The Use of Mouse Models to Study Epigenetics.* November. Accessed January 6, 2020. https://www.ncbi.nlm.nih.gov/pmc/articles/PMC3809579/.

Brimeyer, Tom. 2020. *The 3 Essential Thyroid Diet Rules All Thyroid Sufferers Should Follow (...But Don't).* February 26. Accessed February 28, 2020. https://www.forefronthealth.com/thyroid-diet/.

Cadegiani, Favio A, and Claudio E Kater. 2016. *Adrenal fatigue does not exist: a systematic review.* August 27. Accessed February 27, 2020. https://www.ncbi.nlm.nih.gov/pmc/articles/PMC4997656/.

Campos, Marcelo. 2018 . *Is adrenal fatigue "real"?* February 28. Accessed November 19, 2019. https://www.health.harvard.edu/blog/is-adrenal-fatigue-real-2018022813344.

Carlé, Allan, Inge Bülow Pedersen, Nils Knudsen, Hans Perrild, Lars Ovesen, Lone Banke Rasmussen, Torben Jørgensen, and Peter Laurberg. 2012. *Moderate alcohol consumption may protect against overt autoimmune hypothyroidism: a population-based case–control study.* October. Accessed February 1, 2020. https://eje.bioscientifica.com/view/journals/eje/167/4/483.xml.

Carnahan, Jill. 2015. *Is Toxic Mold Exposure the Cause of Your Symptoms?* February 8. Accessed December 14, 2019. https://www.jillcarnahan.com/2015/02/08/toxic-mold-exposure-cause-symptoms/.

Childs, Westin. 2019. *7 Reasons to Treat Low Ferritin Levels + Step-by-Step Treatment Guide.* February 12. Accessed July 28, 2020. https://www.restartmed.com/low-ferritin/.

Christianson, Alan. 2017. *Is Nigella Sativa The Next "Miracle Herb" for Hashimoto's?* June 2. Accessed December 18, 2019. https://www.youtube.com/watch?v=yENRP0Zg2sc.

Chyka, P.A., and D Seger. 1997. *Position statement: single-dose activated charcoal. American Academy of Clinical Toxicology; European Association of Poisons Centres and Clinical*

Toxicologists. Accessed April 11, 2020. https://pubmed.ncbi.nlm.nih.gov/9482427/.

Cohut, Maria. 2019. *What does science say about the effects of meditation?* March 29. Accessed March 5, 2020. https://www.medicalnewstoday.com/articles/324839.

Cosgrove, Ben. 2015. *The Truth About Detox Diets.* March 19. Accessed April 11, 2020. https://www.berkeleywellness.com/healthy-eating/diet-weight-loss/nutrition/article/truth-about-detox-diets.

Crichton-Stuart, Cathleen. 2018. *How can I tell if I have low magnesium?* June 20. Accessed May 3, 2020. https://www.medicalnewstoday.com/articles/322191.

De Punder, Karin, and Leo Pruimboom. 2013. *The Dietary Intake of Wheat and other Cereal Grains and Their Role in Inflammation.* March. Accessed January 11, 2020. https://www.ncbi.nlm.nih.gov/pmc/articles/PMC3705319/.

Decker, W.J., and D.G. Corby. 1980. *Activated charcoal adsorbs aflatoxin B1.* December. Accessed April 2, 2020. https://pubmed.ncbi.nlm.nih.gov/6782748/.

DerSarkissian, Carol. 2020. *What Kind of Poop Do I Have?* January 16. Accessed April 19, 2020. https://www.webmd.com/digestive-disorders/poop-chart-bristol-stool-scale.

Drutel, Anne, Françoise Archambeaud, and Philippe Caron. 2013. *Selenium and the thyroid gland: more good news for clinicians.* February. Accessed May 9, 2020. https://pubmed.ncbi.nlm.nih.gov/23046013/.

Eshraghian, Ahad, and Alireza Hamidian Jahromi. 2014. *Non-alcoholic fatty liver disease and thyroid dysfunction: A systematic review.* July 7. Accessed November 12, 2019. https://www.ncbi.nlm.nih.gov/pmc/articles/PMC4081681/.

Eske, Jamie. 2019. *How does oxidative stress affect the body?* April 3. Accessed April 2, 2020. https://www.medicalnewstoday.com/articles/324863.

Esposito, Teresa, Jean Marc Lobaccaro, Maria Grazia Esposito, Vincenzo Monda, Antonietta Messina, Giuseppe Paolisso, Bruno Varriale, Marcellino Monda, and Giovanni Messina. 2016. *Effects of low-carbohydrate diet therapy in overweight subjects with autoimmune thyroiditis: possible synergism with ChREBP.* September 14. Accessed February 26, 2020. https://pubmed.ncbi.nlm.nih.gov/27695291/.

Esposito, Teresa, Jean Marc Lobaccaro, Maria Grazia Esposito, Vincenzo Monda, Antonietta Messina, Guiseppe Paolisso, Bruno Varriale, Marcellino Monda, and Giovanni Messina. 2016. *Effects of low-carbohydrate diet therapy in overweight subjects with autoimmune thyroiditis: possible synergism with ChREBP.* September 14. Accessed February 12, 2020. https://www.ncbi.nlm.nih.gov/pmc/articles/PMC5028075/.

Farhangi, Mahdieh Abbasalizad, Parvin Dehghan, and Siroos Tajmiri. 2018. *Powdered black cumin seeds strongly improves serum lipids, atherogenic index of plasma and modulates anthropometric features in patients with Hashimoto's thyroiditis.* March 27. Accessed December 18, 2019. https://www.ncbi.nlm.nih.gov/pmc/articles/PMC5870944/.

Farhangi, Mahdieh Abbasalizad, Parvin Dehghan, Siroos Tajmiri, and Mehran Mesgari Abbasi. 2016. *The effects of Nigella sativa on thyroid function, serum Vascular Endothelial Growth Factor (VEGF) – 1, Nesfatin-1 and anthropometric features in patients with Hashimoto's thyroiditis: a randomized controlled trial.* November 16. Accessed December 18, 2019. https://www.ncbi.nlm.nih.gov/pmc/articles/PMC5112739/.

Franks, Paul W, Soren Brage, Jian'an Luan, Ulf Ekelund, Mushtaquar Rahman, I Sadaf Farooqi, Ian Halsall, Stephen O'Rahilly, and Nicholas J Wareham. 2005. *Leptin predicts a worsening of the features of the metabolic syndrome independently of obesity.* August. Accessed December 20, 2019. https://pubmed.ncbi.nlm.nih.gov/16129731/.

Gavura, Scott. 2017. *Adrenal fatigue: A fake disease (updated).* June 29. Accessed November 19, 2019. https://sciencebasedmedicine.org/adrenal-fatigue-a-fake-disease/.

Genuis, Stephen J, Sanjay Beesoon, Detlef Birkholz, and Rebecca A Lobo. 2011. *Human Excretion of Bisphenol A: Blood, Urine, and Sweat (BUS) Study.* December 27. Accessed March 23, 2020. https://www.hindawi.com/journals/jeph/2012/185731/.

Gunnars, Kris. 2018. *FODMAP 101: A Detailed Beginner's Guide.* November 19. Accessed January 11, 2020. https://www.healthline.com/nutrition/fodmaps-101.

—. 2018. *Mediterranean Diet 101: A Meal Plan and Beginner's Guide.* July 24. Accessed February 27, 2020. https://www.healthline.com/nutrition/mediterranean-diet-meal-plan.

—. 2018. *The Atkins Diet: Everything You Need to Know.* August 2. Accessed February 11, 2020. https://www.healthline.com/nutrition/atkins-diet-101.

Harvard Health. 2013. *The Power of Zzzzs. Uncovering why sleep is essential to our well-being and howto get more of it.* Harvard Health Publications.

Harvard Medical School. 2016. *Hyperthyroidism and your heart.* March. Accessed November 19, 2019. https://www.health.harvard.edu/heart-disease-overview/hyperthyroidism-and-your-heart.

—. 2019. *The lowdown on thyroid slowdown.* March 19. Accessed March 28, 2020. https://www.health.harvard.edu/diseases-and-conditions/the-lowdown-on-thyroid-slowdown.

Health Direct. 2020. *The role of cortisol in the body.* May. Accessed November 16, 2020. https://www.healthdirect.gov.au/the-role-of-cortisol-in-the-body.

Healthline Wellness Team. 2019. *Infrared Saunas: Your Questions Answered.* April 10. Accessed November 27, 2019. https://www.healthline.com/health/under-review-infrared-saunas.

Hedberg, Nicolas. n.d. *Herbal medicines for thyroid disorders.* Accessed November 2, 2019. https://drhedberg.com/herbal-medicines-for-thyroid-disorders/.

Heid, Markham. 2019. *Why You Should Always Wash New Clothes Before Wearing Them.* July 23. Accessed April 10, 2020. https://time.com/5631818/wash-new-clothes/.

Hicklin, Tianna. 2016. *Molecular ties between lack of sleep and weight gain.* March 22. Accessed October 6, 2019. https://www.nih.gov/news-events/nih-research-matters/molecular-ties-between-lack-sleep-weight-gain.

Hormone Health Network. n.d. *Adrenal Fatigue.* Accessed January 20, 2020. https://www.hormone.org/diseases-and-conditions/adrenal-fatigue.

Kalanick, Brooke. n.d. *How To Train If You Have Hypothyroidism or PCOS.* Accessed March 28, 2020. https://www.girlsgonestrong.com/blog/hormones/how-to-modify-your-training-if-you-have-hypothyroidism-or-pcos/?fbclid=IwAR35fqycAj4b-rhuv2GNxHhwhShWYdqc6iakm4mwxIVFfyC3U2xip-oKEJQ.

Kassel, Gabrielle. 2018. *I Worked Out Twice a Day Until It Started Messing With My Hormones.* November 12. Accessed March 27, 2020. https://www.wellandgood.com/exercise-cortisol/.

Kaur, Parvinder, Michael Aschner, and Tore Syversen. 2006. *Glutathione modulation influences methyl mercury induced neurotoxicity in primary cell cultures of neurons and astrocytes.* March 2. Accessed May 18, 2020. https://pubmed.ncbi.nlm.nih.gov/16513172/.

Kharrazian, Dadtis. 2018. *Conversion of T4 to T3 — an important consideration with low thyroid function.* January 9. Accessed February 10, 2020. https://drknews.com/conversion-t4-t3-important-consideration-low-thyroid-function/.

Kharrazian, Datis. 2010. *Changing your diet is the first step in addressing Hashimoto's.* August 9. Accessed February 22, 2020.

https://drknews.com/changing-your-diet-is-the-first-step-in-addressing-hashimotos/.

—. 2018. *Conversion of T4 to T3 — an important consideration with low thyroid function.* January 9. Accessed February 10, 2020. https://drknews.com/conversion-t4-t3-important-consideration-low-thyroid-function/.

—. 2010. *Unraveling thyroid antibody tests.* July 1. Accessed November 18, 2019. https://drknews.com/unraveling-thyroid-antibodies/.

Kharriazian, Dr Datis, interview by Dr Izabella Wentz. n.d. *The Thyroid Secret, Episode 4*

Kidd, Parris. 2003. *Th1/Th2 balance: the hypothesis, its limitations, and implications for health and disease.* August. Accessed October 6, 2019. https://pubmed.ncbi.nlm.nih.gov/12946237/.

Kim, Dohee. 2017. *The Role of Vitamin D in Thyroid Diseases.* September 12. Accessed April 29, 2020. https://pubmed.ncbi.nlm.nih.gov/28895880/.

Kimbrough, Renate D. 1976. *Toxicity and Health Effects of Selected Organotin Compounds: A Review.* May. Accessed March 23, 2020. https://www.researchgate.net/publication/22362210_Toxicity_and_Health_Effects_of_Selected_Organotin_Compounds_A_Review.

Kresser, Chris. 2019. *Exercise and "Adrenal Fatigue".* May 1. Accessed April 20, 2020. https://chriskresser.com/rhr-exercise-and-adrenal-fatigue/.

—. 2018. *Five Thyroid Patterns That Won't Show Up on Standard Lab Tests.* May 9. Accessed November 2, 2020. https://kresserinstitute.com/why-your-normal-thyroid-lab-results-may-not-be-normal/.

—. 2014. *The Truth about Legumes, Saturated Fats, and Vegetarian Diets.* March 12. Accessed January 5, 2020. https://chriskresser.com/the-truth-about-legumes-saturated-fats-and-vegetarian-diets/.

—. 2010. *Why Changing Your Diet Is Always the First Step in Treating Hashimoto's.* August 11. Accessed February 27, 2020. https://chriskresser.com/why-changing-your-diet-is-always-the-first-step-in-treating-hashimotos/.

Levin, L.G., G Iu Mal'tsev, and M.M. Gapparov. 1978. *Effect of thiamine deficiency in hydrochloric acid secretion in the stomach.* Sept-Oct. Accessed May 4, 2020. https://pubmed.ncbi.nlm.nih.gov/716330/.

Levy, Jillian. 2019. *The Top Zinc Benefits to Improve Health & How to Regulate Levels.* May 10. Accessed March 29, 2020. https://draxe.com/nutrition/zinc-benefits/.

—. 2018. *What Is Betaine? Benefits, Signs of Deficiency and Food Sources.* October 24. Accessed May 18, 2020. https://draxe.com/nutrition/what-is-betaine/.

Lindemann, Bella. 2016. *Eating for IBS: How to Choose the Best Diet for You.* November 23. Accessed February 22, 2020. https://bellalindemann.com/blog/eating-ibs-choose-diet.

Link, Rachael. 2018. *The Vegetarian Diet: A Beginner's Guide and Meal Plan.* October 17. Accessed February 25, 2020. https://www.healthline.com/nutrition/vegetarian-diet-plan.

MacMillan, Amanda. 2015. *13 Ways Inflammation Can Affect Your Health.* March 4. Accessed February 5, 2020. https://www.health.com/mind-body/13-ways-inflammation-can-affect-your-health.

Mandal, Ananya. 2019. *What are Cytokines?* February 26. Accessed November 28, 2019. https://www.news-medical.net/health/What-are-Cytokines.aspx.

Matthias, T, P Jeremias, S Neidhöfer, and A Lerner. 2016. *The industrial food additive, microbial transglutaminase, mimics tissue transglutaminase and is immunogenic in celiac disease patients.* September 15. Accessed February 10, 2020. https://pubmed.ncbi.nlm.nih.gov/27640315/.

Mayo Clinic Staff. s.d. *Hypothyroidism (underactive thyroid).* Accessed November 2019.

—. 2019. *Mediterranean diet: A heart-healthy eating plan.* June 21. Accessed February 27, 2020. https://www.mayoclinic.org/healthy-lifestyle/nutrition-and-healthy-eating/in-depth/mediterranean-diet/art-20047801.

—. n.d. *Zinc.* Accessed May 18, 2020. https://www.mayoclinic.org/drugs-supplements-zinc/art-20366112.

Merriam-Webster Dictionary. n.d. *Adaptogen.* Accessed December 10, 2019. https://www.merriam-webster.com/dictionary/adaptogen.

Mokhtari, Vida, Parvaneh Afsharian, Maryam Shahhoseini, Seyed Mehdi Kalantar, and Ashraf Moini. 2016. *A Review on Various Uses of N-Acetyl Cysteine.* December 21. Accessed May 19, 2020. https://www.ncbi.nlm.nih.gov/pmc/articles/PMC5241507/.

Myers, Amy. 2019. February 19. Accessed January 3, 2020. https://www.amymyersmd.com/2019/02/foods-you-should-never-eat/ .

—. 2018. *3 Important reaons to give up gluten if you have an autoimmune disease.* April 17. Accessed December 14, 2019. https://www.amymyersmd.com/article/give-up-gluten-autoimmune-disease/.

—. 2017. *6 Benefits of Infrared Sauna Therapy.* September 23. Accessed March 10, 2020. https://www.amymyersmd.com/article/benefits-infrared-sauna-therapy/.

—. 2015. *The Autoimmune Solution Pillar IV: Heal Your Infections and Relieve Your Stress.* March 20. Accessed November 20, 2019. https://www.amymyersmd.com/2015/03/the-autoimmune-solution-pillar-iv-heal-your-infections-and-relieve-your-stress/.

—. 2017. *Understanding the true cause of autoimmune disease.* January 24. Accessed December 3, 2019. https://www.amymyersmd.com/2017/01/understanding-true-cause-autoimmune-disease/.

N. n.d. *Benfotiamine.* Accessed May 8, 2020. https://www.nhc.com/benfotiamine.

N. n.d. *Cardio Exercise.* Ebook, Harvard Medical School. Accessed March 24, 2020. https://www.health.harvard.edu/exercise-and-fitness/cardio-exercise.

—. 2018. *Dietary supplements: Dubious value, hidden dangers.* December. Accessed April 28, 2020. https://www.health.harvard.edu/heart-health/dietary-supplements-dubious-value-hidden-dangers.

—. 2019. *How does the immune system work?* November 2019. Accessed January 6, 2020. https://www.ncbi.nlm.nih.gov/books/NBK279364/.

—. 2019. "Mindful Eating." *Lose It Magazine*, April 30: 25-27.

—. 2020. *Magnesium.* March 24. Accessed May 4, 2020. https://ods.od.nih.gov/factsheets/Magnesium-HealthProfessional/.

—. n.d. *Manganese.* Accessed May 8, 2020. https://www.webmd.com/vitamins/ai/ingredientmono-182/manganese.

—. n.d. *Organotin Compound.* Accessed March 28, 2020. https://www.sciencedirect.com/topics/pharmacology-toxicology-and-pharmaceutical-science/organotin-compound.

—. n.d. *Phases of detox.* Accessed April 12, 2020. https://www.cincinnatihealthinstitute.com/Articles.asp?ID=321.

—. 2016. *The Four Shades of B12 IVs and Shots.* September 28. Accessed May 10, 2020. https://revivme.com/the-four-shades-of-b12-ivs-and-shots/.

—. 2020. *Vitamin B12.* March 30. Accessed May 9, 2020. https://ods.od.nih.gov/factsheets/VitaminB12-Consumer/.

—. n.d. *Vitamin B12 Oral.* Accessed May 9, 2020. https://my.clevelandclinic.org/health/drugs/20271-vitamin-b12-oral.

—. 2019. *Vitamin D Deficiency.* October 16. Accessed May 12, 2020. https://my.clevelandclinic.org/health/articles/15050-vitamin-d--vitamin-d-deficiency.

—. n.d. *Vitamin E: What You Need to Know.* Accessed April 30, 2020. https://www.webmd.com/diet/ss/slideshow-vitamin-e-guide.

—. n.d. *Vitamin E: What's It Good For?* Accessed April 30, 2020. https://www.webmd.com/vitamins-and-supplements/ss/slideshow-vitamin-e-benefits.

—. n.d. *What is a Ferritin Blood Test?* Accessed May 4, 2020. https://www.webmd.com/a-to-z-guides/ferritin-blood-test#1.

—. 2018. *What You Should Know About Medicines/Sublingual.* August 19. Accessed May 10, 2020. https://en.wikibooks.org/wiki/What_You_Should_Know_About_Medicines/Sublingual.

Naiman, Rubin. 2011. *Turn On, Tune In, Nod Out: A Mindful Approach to Sleep - Part 2.* August 10. Accessed March 3, 2020. https://www.psychologytoday.com/us/blog/mindful-sleep-mindful-dreams/201108/turn-tune-in-nod-out-mindful-approach-sleep-part-2.

Niemiec, Ryan M. 2017. *10 New Strategies for Stress Management.* January 19. Accessed August 16, 2020.

https://www.psychologytoday.com/us/blog/what-matters-most/201701/10-new-strategies-stress-management.

Norman, James. 2021. *Hypothyroidism: Overview, Causes, and Symptoms.* February 17. Accessed February 20, 2021. https://www.endocrineweb.com/conditions/thyroid/hypothyroidism-too-little-thyroid-hormone.

Osansky, Eric. 2014. *Thyroid Health Tip: What Type Of Diet Should You Follow?* September 11. Accessed February 28, 2020. https://www.naturalendocrinesolutions.com/thyroid-health-tip-what-type-of-diet-should-you-follow/.

—. 2012. *Vitamin A and Thyroid Health.* November 26. Accessed May 28, 2020. https://www.naturalendocrinesolutions.com/articles/vitamin-a-thyroid-health/.

Oto, Brandon. 2012. *When thinking is hard: managing decision fatigue.* May. Accessed December 5, 2019. https://www.researchgate.net/publication/225279309_When_thinking_is_hard_managing_decision_fatigue.

PaleoLeap. n.d. *All about nightshades.* Accessed January 10, 2020. https://paleoleap.com/nightshades/.

Palmer, Sharon. 2013. *The Mediterranean Diet — An Up-Close Look at Its Origins in Pantelleria.* May. Accessed February 27, 2020. https://www.todaysdietitian.com/newarchives/050113p28.shtml.

Pang, Qihau, Yanru Li, Lingxue Meng, Guanyong Li, Zhiwei Luo, and Ruifang Fan. 2019. *Neurotoxicity of BPA, BPS, and BPB for the hippocampal cell line (HT-22): An implication for the replacement of BPA in plastics.* March 30. Accessed November 22, 2019. https://pubmed.ncbi.nlm.nih.gov/30953899/.

Paris, Laura. 2017. *Functional Medicine Detox Phases 1, 2, and 3.* April 16. Accessed April 19, 2020. https://www.parishealingarts.com/functional-medicine-phase-detox/.

Perlmutter, David. n.d. *Gluten Containing Products.* Accessed January 3, 2020. https://www.drperlmutter.com/eat/foods-that-contain-gluten/.

Petre, Alina. 2016. *11 Foods Healthy Vegans Eat.* October 14. Accessed February 8, 2020. https://www.healthline.com/nutrition/foods-vegans-eat.

Purse, Marcia. 2019. *Overview of Your Medication's Half-Life.* September 29. Accessed December 12, 2019. https://www.verywellmind.com/medication-half-life-380031.

Pusztai, A, and G Grant. 1998. *Assessment of lectin inactivation by heat and digestion.* Accessed January 4, 2020. https://pubmed.ncbi.nlm.nih.gov/21374488/.

Rathnavelu, Vidhya, Noorjahan Banu Alitheen, Subramaniam Sohila, Samikannu Kanagesan, and Rajendran Ramesh. 2016. *Potential role of bromelain in clinical and therapeutic applications.* July 18. Accessed May 20, 2020. https://www.ncbi.nlm.nih.gov/pmc/articles/PMC4998156/.

Ratini, Melinda. 2019. *Selenium.* March 26. Accessed May 6, 2020. https://www.webmd.com/a-to-z-guides/supplement-guide-selenium#1.

Rekstis, Emily. 2019. *Poop and you.* May 17. Accessed April 19, 2020. https://www.healthline.com/health/digestive-health/types-of-poop.

Robbins, Ocean. 2019. *Safe and Healthy Cookware: What You Need To Know When Choosing Non-Toxic Pots & Pans.* August 23. Accessed March 20, 2020. https://foodrevolution.org/blog/healthy-cookware/.

Robertson, Ruairi. 2020. *Omega-3-6-9 Fatty Acids: A Complete Overview.* October 22. Accessed December 20, 2020. https://www.healthline.com/nutrition/omega-3-6-9-overview.

Romeo, Javier, Julia Wärnberg, Esther Nova, Ligia E Díaz, Sonia Gómez-Martinez, and Ascensión Marcos. 2007. *Moderate alcohol consumption and the immune system: A review.* October 1. Accessed February 1, 2020. https://www.cambridge.org/core/journals/british-journal-of-nutrition/article/moderate-alcohol-consumption-and-the-immune-system-a-review/D340A16DDC772F6F2625001BD4AD430B.

Ruggeri, Christine. 2018. *Vitamin B12 Benefits That You're Probably Missing.* September 28. Accessed May 8, 2020. https://draxe.com/nutrition/vitamin-b12-benefits/.

Runyon, Joel. 2019. *The Ultimate Paleo Diet Food List.* May 1. Accessed February 8, 2020. https://ultimatepaleoguide.com/paleo-diet-food-list/.

Sampson, Stacy. 2018. *Is adrenal fatigue a real condition?* June 27. Accessed August 16, 2020. https://www.medicalnewstoday.com/articles/245810.

Seaman, Greg. 2012. *Plastics by the Numbers.* May 2. Accessed March 28, 2020. https://learn.eartheasy.com/articles/plastics-by-the-numbers/.

Sears, Margaret E. 2013. *Chelation: Harnessing and Enhancing Heavy Metal Detoxification—A Review.* April 18. Accessed March 28, 2020. https://www.ncbi.nlm.nih.gov/pmc/articles/PMC3654245/#B20.

Sears, Margaret E, Kathleen J Kerr, and Riina I Bray. 2012. *Arsenic, Cadmium, Lead, and Mercury in Sweat: A Systematic Review.* February 22. Accessed March 23, 2020. https://www.hindawi.com/journals/jeph/2012/184745/#B30.

Seligman, M.E.P, T.A. Steen, N Park, and C Peterson. 2005. "Positive psychology progress: Empirical validation of interventions." *American Psychologist* 410-421.

Shomon, Mary. 2019. *Treating Thyroid Disease With Triiodothyronine (T3) Drugs.* November 25. Accessed January 10, 2020.

Sibiya, Inga. n.d. *WHAT'S THE DEAL WITH ESSENTIAL OILS?* Accessed March 6, 2020. https://www.faithful-to-nature.co.za/blog/whats-the-deal-with-essential-oils/.

Society for Endocrinology. 2018. *Calcitonin.* February. Accessed November 2019. https://www.yourhormones.info/hormones/calcitonin/.

Staff, Mayo Clinic. 2019. *Chronic stress puts your health at risk.* March 19. Accessed November 24, 2019.

https://www.mayoclinic.org/healthy-lifestyle/stress-management/in-depth/stress/art-20046037.

Steelsmith, Laurie. 2018. *Which is the Best Type of Magnesium for You?* April 4. Accessed May 6, 2020. https://www.vitacost.com/blog/types-of-magnesium/.

Storoni, Mithu, and Gordon T Plant. 2015. *The Therapeutic Potential of the Ketogenic Diet in Treating Progressive Multiple Sclerosis.* December 29. Accessed February 10, 2020. https://www.ncbi.nlm.nih.gov/pmc/articles/PMC4709725/.

Sugar Science. n.d. *Hidden in Plain Sight.* Accessed January 12, 2020. http://sugarscience.ucsf.edu/hidden-in-plain-sight/#.YFCJtp0zZPZ.

Tonstad, Serena, Edward Nathan, Keiji Oda, and Gary Fraser. 2013. *Vegan Diets and Hypothyroidism.* November 13. Accessed February 25, 2020. https://www.ncbi.nlm.nih.gov/pmc/articles/PMC3847753/.

Topiler, Ina. 2019. *Are you making one of these 5 classic mistakes in the name of health?* November 21. Accessed March 12, 2020. https://healthmysteriessolved.com/health-traps-become-health-mysteries/.

Torsten, Matthias, and Lerner Aaron. 2018. *Microbial Transglutaminase Is Immunogenic and Potentially Pathogenic in Pediatric Celiac Disease.* December 11. Accessed January 10, 2020. https://www.ncbi.nlm.nih.gov/pmc/articles/PMC6297833/.

Trentini, Dana. 2018. *5 reasons conventional doctors can't fix your thyroid.* May 7. Accessed November 22, 2019.

https://hypothyroidmom.com/5-reasons-conventional-doctors-cant-fix-your-thyroid/#more-13978.

—. 2015. *Autoimmune Patients, Have You Heard of Th1 and Th2 Dominance?* March 22. Accessed October 25, 2020. https://hypothyroidmom.com/autoimmune-patients-have-you-heard-of-th1-and-th2-dominance/.

—. 2018. *Understanding the True Cause of Autoimmune Disease.* May 1. Accessed March 6, 2020. https://hypothyroidmom.com/understanding-the-true-cause-of-autoimmune-disease/.

—. 2018. *Understanding the True Cause of Autoimmune Disease.* May 1. Accessed January 16, 2020. https://hypothyroidmom.com/understanding-the-true-cause-of-autoimmune-disease/.

—. 2017. *Why Caring for Your Liver is Key to Healing from Hashimoto's.* April 3. Accessed November 18, 2019. https://hypothyroidmom.com/why-caring-for-your-liver-is-key-to-healing-from-hashimotos/.

Ucan, Bekir, Mustafa Sahin, Muyesser Sayki Arslan, Nujen Colak Bozkurt, Muhammed Kizilgul, Askin Güngünes , Erman Cakal, and Mustafa Ozbek. 2017. *Vitamin D Treatment in Patients with Hashimoto's Thyroiditis may Decrease the Development of Hypothyroidism.* July 12. Accessed April 28, 2020. https://pubmed.ncbi.nlm.nih.gov/28697689/.

Villines, Zawn. 2017. July 29. Accessed April 5, 2020. https://www.medicalnewstoday.com/articles/318652.

—. 2017. *What is the best type of meditation?* December 22. Accessed March 4, 2020. https://www.medicalnewstoday.com/articles/320392.

Wang, H Joe, Samir Zakhari, and M Katherine Jung. 2010. *Alcohol, inflammation, and gut-liver-brain interactions in tissue damage and disease development.* March 21. Accessed February 2, 2020. https://www.ncbi.nlm.nih.gov/pmc/articles/PMC2842521/.

Ware, Megan. 2018. *Selenium: What it does and how much you need.* January 12. Accessed May 8, 2020. https://www.medicalnewstoday.com/articles/287842.

Wentz, Isabella. 2017. *Hashimoto's Protocol: A 90 Day Plan for Reversing Thyroid Symptoms and Getting Your Life Back.* HarperOne.

Wentz, Izabella. 2017. *Adverse Reactions to Helpful Supplements.* October 13. Accessed November 12, 2019. https://thyroidpharmacist.com/articles/support-liver-recover-from-thyroid-disease/.

—. 2018. *Get Some Sunshine For Your Thyroid!* March 23. Accessed March 28, 2020. https://thyroidpharmacist.com/articles/get-some-sunshine-for-your-thyroid/.

—. 2019. *How Avoiding Soy Can Benefit Hashimoto's.* February 15. Accessed December 19, 2019. https://thyroidpharmacist.com/articles/soy-and-hashimotos/.

—. 2017. *How To Get Accurate Lab Tests When Taking Thyroid Medications.* September 29. Accessed December 8, 2019.

https://thyroidpharmacist.com/articles/how-to-get-accurate-lab-tests-when-taking-thyroid-medications/.

—. 2018. *How to lose weight with Hashimoto's.* January 20. Accessed January 23, 2020. https://thyroidpharmacist.com/articles/how-to-lose-weight-with-hashimotos/.

—. 2019. *How Vitamin E Impacts Your Thyroid.* March 7. Accessed May 2, 2020. https://thyroidpharmacist.com/articles/vitamin-e-and-hashimotos/.

—. 2019. *How Vitamin E Impacts Your Thyroid.* March 07. Accessed May 8, 2020. https://thyroidpharmacist.com/articles/vitamin-e-and-hashimotos/.

—. 2017. *Iodine and Hashimoto's.* May 6. Accessed December 7, 2019. https://thyroidpharmacist.com/articles/iodine-hashimotos/.

—. 2019. *Studies on Magnesium and Thyroid Health.* October 17. Accessed May 2, 2020. https://thyroidpharmacist.com/articles/new-studies-on-magnesium-and-thyroid-health/.

—. 2020. *The 5 Stages of Hashimoto's Thyroiditis.* August 06. Accessed October 28, 2020 . https://thyroidpharmacist.com/articles/5-stages-hashimotos-thyroiditis/.

—. 2020. *The 7 Most Common Nutrient Deficiencies in Hashimoto's.* January 9. Accessed May 2, 2020. https://thyroidpharmacist.com/articles/most-common-nutrient-deficiencies-hashimotos/.

—. 2020. *The Surprising Effect of Zinc Deficiency on Hashimoto's.* April 22. Accessed May 18, 2020. https://thyroidpharmacist.com/articles/hashimotos-and-zinc-deficiency/.

—. 2020. *Thiamine and Thyroid Fatigue.* February 20. Accessed May 4, 2020. https://thyroidpharmacist.com/articles/thiamine-and-thyroid-fatigue/.

—. 2018. *Top 7 Hashimoto's Food Myths.* September 13. Accessed February 26, 2020. https://thyroidpharmacist.com/articles/top-7-hashimotos-food-myths/.

—. 2019. *Turmeric for Your Thyroid and Hashimoto's.* September 12. Accessed May 28, 2020. https://thyroidpharmacist.com/articles/turmeric-for-your-thyroid-and-hashimotos/.

—. 2017. *Using Enzymes to Overcome Hashimoto's.* November 10. Accessed May 27, 2020. https://thyroidpharmacist.com/articles/using-enzymes-to-overcome-hashimotos/.

—. 2018. *What Are Goitrogens and Do They Matter with Hashimoto's?* August 16. Accessed February 18, 2020. https://thyroidpharmacist.com/articles/what-are-goitrogens-and-do-they-matter-with-hashimotos/.

West, Helen. 2019. *What Are Essential Oils, and Do They Work?* September 30. Accessed March 6, 2020. https://www.healthline.com/nutrition/what-are-essential-oils.

What is Epigenetics. 2018. *A Super Brief and Basic Explanation of Epigenetics for Total Beginners.* July 30. Accessed November

28, 2019. https://www.whatisepigenetics.com/what-is-epigenetics/.

Whelan, Corey. 2020. *Bromelain.* April 21. Accessed May 28, 2020. https://www.healthline.com/health/bromelain.

Wilson, Debra Rose. 2018. *Why You Should Avoid Adrenal Extract.* September 17. Accessed August 16, 2020. https://www.healthline.com/health/why-you-should-avoid-adrenal-extract.

Yasir, Muhammad, Amandeep Goyal, Pankaj Bansal, and Sidharth Sonthalia. 2020. *Corticosteroid Adverse Effects.* July 4. Accessed August 14, 2020. https://www.ncbi.nlm.nih.gov/books/NBK531462/.

You and Your Hormones. 2019. *Cortisol.* January. Accessed February 5, 2020. https://www.yourhormones.info/hormones/cortisol/.

Zeevalk, Gail D, Laura P Bernard, and F.T. Guilford. 2010. *Liposomal-glutathione provides maintenance of intracellular glutathione and neuroprotection in mesencephalic neuronal cells.* June 10. Accessed May 20, 2020. https://pubmed.ncbi.nlm.nih.gov/20535554/.

Printed in Great Britain
by Amazon

68619961R00189